Customer Service Communication Library
Volume 1

Harness the Power of Exceptional Customer Service

Essential People Skills to Make Profits Soar

By
Gaylyn Williams

Outskirts Press, Inc.
Denver, CO

This book is available at special quantity discounts to use for sales promotions or for business staff. To order or for more information, please contact us at:

Phone: 800-788-9171
Email: Sales@SuccessBooks.info
Website: www.SuccessBooks.info
Address: Success Books, LLC
          P.O. Box 63383
          Colorado Springs, CO 80962

Endorsements

"If you want to transform your business and multiply your profits ... you must put the relationship before the transaction. I know of no more effective author on the subject of interpersonal skills than Gaylyn Williams. Before you spend a nickel on another 'how to' book on ... techniques or tactics—harness the power of communication!"
—**Paul Strauss,** *President of WCRT, Chicago, IL*

"Gaylyn is a pro. Her products are well-thought out, informative, and a pleasure to read. The world needs more mentors like this. Keep up the good work."
—**Claude Diamond,** *Mentor/Author/Speaker, The Lease Purchase Success Kit, How to Coach, Consult, and Mentor, San Diego, CA*

"*A must read* for every person who will interact with customers. ...*A must read* for those without prior experience in sales and management. *A must read* for those wanting the ultimate result from any relationship, business or personal. Of the books, tapes and CDs I have acquired over the past thirty years, Gaylyn has given **us what I consider the most powerful tool** to date."
—**Jim Werner**, *30-year Business Owner, Fort Myers, FL*

"Good communication skills are an indispensable tool for your success. Gaylyn has written a timeless book, with numerous insights, hints, secrets and skills you can put into practice immediately to achieve maximum results in your business. This series is an absolute essential for everyone wanting to maximize the profit potential in business."
—**William Bronchick**, Attorney & Best-Selling Author

"This book is long overdue... the problem is never making money: It is knowing how to keep it and how to deal with people and problems, and people problems. What a great tool!"
—**Bill J. Gatten,** *Author, Business Owner, West Hills, CA*

"An extremely well put together book with everything you need to know about top-notch customer service. Gaylyn Williams hits the nail right on the head and pounds it home time and time again with the many tools, tips and strategies written in this book."
—**Ben Harris,** *Chick-Fil-A, Colorado Springs, CO*

"I use the skills I learned in the Customer Service Communication Library every single day as I answer calls from people wanting to cancel their phone service. The skills have helped me be more effective in my job and get more bonuses."
—**Jonathan Whalin**, *Customer-service Representative for Qwest Communications*

"Having started in the business world at an early age, it became clear to me how important relationships are in every situation. Those that understood this were successful. Gaylyn 'hits the nail on the head' with her studies on the *relationship* taking a precedent in any business! This is a *must read* for anyone looking for a solid base to begin their business and/or a new perspective in a customer-based position. Easy-to-read, easy-to-follow and most of all—easy to implement!"
—**David W. Lewis**, *AVP, Wholesale Technology Marketing Manager for American Brokers Conduit, Denver, CO*

"This course is excellent for anyone owning or working in a business. People skills and customer service are the keys to business success and this manual clearly outlines how to do that. What a treasure!"
—**Joanne Moeller**, *Director for Franciscan Retreat Center, Colorado Springs, CO*

"Life is lived in relationships with other people. Some are close and personal, some are not, but all require an amazing assortment of skills if those relationships are to be positive. This course takes a clear and practical look at the major areas that are so critical to any healthy relationship. I have attended my share of 'how-to' sessions designed to improve various facets of my work skills. Rarely have I taken away something I use every single day. I use the tools given in this book in every relationship."
—**Tim Westcott**, Southern California

Table of Contents

Acknowledgments

I would like to say a special thank you to the following people. Without them, this book would not be possible.

Ken L. Williams, PhD. This book is based on Dr. Williams' (my father) research and study from his doctoral studies in human behavior and years of counseling and training with nonprofit leaders around the world.

My sons, Jonathan and Timothy Whalin. As a single mom, I've had many opportunities to practice and refine my interpersonal skills. Thank you, Jon and Timothy, for your love and patience with me as I have spent hours researching, writing and practicing these skills with you.

My writers group: Colleen Shine and Linda Harris. I couldn't have finished this book without your invaluable insights. You have gone over each chapter in this book at least once. You are also an encouragement and inspiration to me.

Introduction

"Very few sales people and entrepreneurs discover early enough that...the most important skills for success include mastering the strategies for building relationships, influencing others, handling conflicts, and creating credibility."
Richard Roop, Author, Speaker, Business Owner
Bottom Line Results, www.RichardRoop.com, 1-877-932-9725

What *Exceptional Customer Service* Will Do for You

This interactive course is designed to help anyone who interacts with the public to become more effective in influencing and communicating with customers, prospects, and business associates.

This course equips you with the skills needed to build a firm foundation for your job, career or business. Just as a house needs a strong foundation—your job, career or business needs one to survive and thrive. People skills are essential to every part of your business. Everything you do as a salesperson or customer-service representative involves people. You will learn how to:

- Develop effective communication skills to increase your success

- Relate to prospective customers in a manner that shows you can be trusted to help solve their problems

- Figure out what the customer really wants and why

- Build rapport with customers and business associates quickly

- Create receptivity for your sales approach, so you can communicate to seal the deal

- Establish a bond of trust resulting in return sales and referrals

- Be more effective in your negotiations and sales presentations

- Read your customer's nonverbal communication to make the sale

Note: For simplicity, masculine pronouns designate both genders.

Why Develop Exceptional Communication Skills?

Contrary to what many people think, technology doesn't make or break your customer service reputation. It's the people behind the technology who make or break your profits. If your customer-service representatives aren't trained properly, great products, technology or services won't matter much.

> **Superior customer service is one of the best ways to stand out from the competition.**
> **Your staff must be able to resolve customer problems promptly and successfully.**

How many businesses promote their technology, products or services, yet forget about people? Retaining current customers is a lot less expensive than obtaining new ones.

So...How Do You Keep Customers Coming Back?

This interactive manual provides the tools and skill training to retain current customers and also bring in new customers through word of mouth.

> **"Most entrepreneurs dramatically overestimate their people skills.**
> **That overconfidence can be a fatal business flaw.**
> **The entrepreneurs who get ahead are those with good people skills."**
> **Frank Shipper, a business professor at Salisbury State University in Maryland**

If you provide the best service in town, many customers will give you their business—regardless of the cost. You can differentiate your products or services through superior customer service, but it will not happen overnight.

With a million things to think about, entrepreneurs work extremely hard to get a business off the ground. If you're looking to distinguish your business and offer the competitive advantage, then focus on customer service. This path has to be a long-term strategy. It will take patience to see the results.

> ## Good service is extremely hard to find.

Many business people think: "Price is everything." This is not always true. People pay more when you give them more. If you establish a reputation for service, great things will happen. It will be easier to—

- gain new customers
- obtain more business from existing customers
- increase your prices

Internal Versus External Customer Service

When you think of customer service, do you only think about "external customer service"—how you relate to your customers? External customer service is very important, but "internal customer service" is equally important.

"Internal customer service" serves fellow employees and other departments within our organizations, as well as suppliers and others with whom we work to accomplish our jobs. Happy employees equal happy customers.

> ## Employee satisfaction equals customer satisfaction.

Many companies' mission statements, motivational seminars, business courses, books, and articles talk about the importance of exceptional customer service. Yet, many businesses fail to recognize that the principal path to exceptional customer service is through internal customer service.

Some important questions to ask include:

- How do you greet a fellow employee who walks into your office needing to talk?

- How do you treat a colleague who asks for information to complete a task?

- How do you react when someone from marketing asks for addresses of good contacts?

These things can be seen as interruptions that take you away from your "real" jobs, yet they are vital to your company's success. In helping others in your company, you help your company succeed.

> **37 percent of workers noted**
> **the most important quality in a boss is good interpersonal skills,**
> **according to a survey conducted by Personnel Decisions International (PDI).**
> **And that attitude impacts the bottom line.**

"Caring for your 'associates' is fundamental to caring for your customers and shareholders," says Arthur M. Blank, co-founder of Home Depot. Superior internal customer service improves morale, productivity, employee retention, external customer service, and ultimately, profitability.

The following "internal customer service" steps will ensure your customers receive exceptional service:

1. Develop a way to measure superb customer service in your company.

2. Reward employees who consistently practice good customer-service skills.

3. Ensure excellent customer service runs rampant throughout your company.

4. Show employees how good service relates to your profits and to their futures with the company.

5. Commit to providing more exceptional customer service than anyone else in your industry.

> **Helping others helps your company succeed.**

Which skills are essential to sustain the growth of a business? According to David Goldsmith, a management coach in Orlando, Florida, the four key skills are:

1. **Communication**—Is your vision understandable?

2. **Listening**—Do you hear and respond to the feedback your employees and customers provide?

3. **Compassion**—Do you understand how your customers as well as employees feel?

4. **Attitude**—Do you respect your employees and customers?

> You need good communication skills to deal with
> your team, employees, vendors, customers, and investors.
> How you communicate often leaves more of an impression on people
> than what you've said.
> Spend the time to develop strong communication skills,
> and you'll greatly boost your chances for success.

Tim Fulton, a consultant with the Small Business Development Center at Clayton State College in Morrow, Georgia, recommends the following when you recognize the need to improve customer-service skills:

1. List the people skills needed in your business.

2. Honestly rate your people skills.

3. Polish the skills that need buffing. The key to improving is to keep practicing.

This manual will walk you through each of these steps.

Lack of customer-service skills is a real problem business owners face. The problem often sneaks up on you. When your staff is small, difficulties don't often surface at first. As your business grows, problems arise because many people lack the basic communication skills needed.

What is the problem? Few business owners get where they are by virtue of exceptional interpersonal or customer-service skills. Many people go into business because they:
- have strong technical abilities
- are talented sales persons
- cannot tolerate working for others

Very few entrepreneurs start businesses because they get along well with people. Starting and running a business is not easy, but long-term success will be dramatically enhanced when you learn exceptional customer-service communication skills. This manual is a good place to start to effectively learn and practice people skills.

Success Builders International provides practical, interactive customer-service communication skills workshops, designed to empower businesses to maximum success. These workshops are essential for:

- Salespeople
- Supervisors
- All employees
- Business owners
- Upper-level managers
- Customer-service representatives
- *Anyone* who interfaces with the public

For more information contact Success Builders International:
Email: info@SuccessBooks.info
Web Site: www.SuccessBooks.info

If you provide the best customer service in town many customers will give you their business —regardless of the cost.

Ways This Series Will Increase Your Profit$

1. *Multiply your income exponentially.* The number-one way to increase your bottom line is to maximize your ability to communicate with people.

2. *Teach you to partner productively with customers who are difficult or face difficulty.* Learn how to empathize with people considering a purchase. Your understanding and skill will gain client trust and reward your business or career.

3. *Turn conflict into profit.* The typical customer-service representative or customer either avoids or reacts poorly to conflict. Exceptional customer service handles conflict well, builds loyal customers and increases word of mouth referrals.

4. *Build your reputation.* Exceptional customer-service skills guarantee a top-rate reputation.

5. *Help you to become known as a problem solver.* Learn how to help prospects and customers effectively solve problems.

6. *De-stress your life to keep you in business for the long haul.* Discover ways to prioritize and maintain balance in your personal and professional life.

7. *Crash-proof your career or business.* You will learn ways to communicate in your job, career or business so you stand head and shoulders above others. Your honesty, integrity and ethics secure your position against mistakes or moral missteps.

8. *Train your employees.* When your employees have exceptional customer-service communication skills, they will be more successful and you make more money.

> **People skills are much more important than most people realize.**

About the Author

Gaylyn Williams has written and published fourteen books, including one published by *Reader's Digest.* Her books are translated in fifteen languages. She is an international speaker and seminar trainer for communication and people skills. As CEO of Success Builders International in Colorado Springs, CO, she applies the customer-service skills in this manual daily with inside and outside customers.

Gaylyn served on the board for the Colorado Springs Customer Service Association and Pikes Peak Landlord and Investor's Group. She is the executive director of Relationship Resources, Inc., a nonprofit corporation. As a certified facilitator and trainer with International Training Partners, she taught communication skills workshops for many organizations, including the Department of Human Services, Colorado Springs Customer Service Association, Child Support Services, Pikes Peak Workforce Center, and English Language Institute China (in Thailand). She has conducted training for numerous nonprofits, for-profit businesses, churches, and retreats. Some of the countries where she has facilitated communication seminars include the United States, Mexico, Thailand, France, Jordan, and Cyprus. Gaylyn is a member of the Southern Colorado Better Business Bureau, Colorado Springs Association of Real Estate Investors, and Colorado Association of Real Estate Investors.

See Appendix E for more books written by Gaylyn Williams.

Author's Story
Struggling Single Mom Becomes Successful Business Owner

Gaylyn went from being an impoverished single mom to becoming a successful business owner in three-and-a-half years. After graduating from college with a bachelor's degree in linguistics, she married and moved to Guatemala. Gaylyn worked with Wycliffe Bible Translators for fifteen years as a linguist, teacher, researcher, writer, and editor.

Then life brought drastic changes. As a single mom raising two sons alone, she struggled to pay bills. Gaylyn had no idea what to do. She only knew that more than anything else, she wanted to be a mom to her boys. Gaylyn began searching for a business to conduct successfully from home. Her first home business created stained glass windows and stenciled people's walls, lamps and furniture.

Gaylyn also wanted to help other single-parent families in the Colorado Springs area. To do so, she started Parenting Solo Network, a nonprofit dedicated to helping these families practically, educationally, emotionally, and socially. She facilitated single-parent groups, planned weekly family activities, helped in practical ways, and ran a food bank out of her garage.

After attending a *Sharpening Your Interpersonal Skills* workshop in 1997, Gaylyn decided to venture out to start a new business. She launched Relationship Resources, a nonprofit corporation dedicated to providing quality books and communication training to nonprofit leaders internationally.

In 2003 Gaylyn started Success Builders International, a for profit corporation, providing books, training and coaching for business owners and customer-service representatives. She also runs her own real estate investment business.

Gaylyn is an expert at showing people how to close more deals by utilizing exceptional customer-service skills. As an international speaker and communication trainer, she has helped thousands of people worldwide to learn how to communicate more effectively.

What This Package Includes

To develop effective communication skills in your business career, study each section and complete the assignments. This interactive workbook includes:

Key Concept Articles: Offers useful methods to apply exceptional customer-service communication secrets to increase career or business success.

True-to-Life Customer-Service Examples: Presents common customer-service situations and their profitable outcomes.

Self-Assessment Tools: Evaluates your communication habits and provides behavior-altering insights.

Motivational Quotes: Reinforces insights to increase customer-service abilities.

Activities: Integrates knowledge and skills to change habits of thinking to produce consistently effective communication.

Case Studies: Proposes real-life situations to rehearse to reinforce effective responses.

Snapshots: Furnishes a place to record specific skills to practice and master from chapter content.

Opportunities for Growth: Offers extra ideas to enhance all your relationships—personally and professionally.

An Optional Training DVD: A dramatic vignette illustrates each communication skill and provides a practical opportunity to practice each skill.

Core Beliefs Dramatically Affect Your Profits

Many core beliefs form the foundation of this workbook. A core belief is defined as:

A firmly held conviction that consistently motivates my behavior.

Belief + Consistent Action = Core Belief

A belief is something you say you believe. However, a core belief is not only what you state you believe, but how you act *most of the time.* Much of what you think and feel about life, yourself and others is based on your core beliefs.

Core beliefs regarding communication affect the success or failure of your relationships and business. The *Customer Service Communication Library* will help you discover beliefs that limit your potential to build rewarding relationships in your job, career, business, or personal life.

> **This book contains thoroughly road-tested, step-by-step skills and learning methods to make you more successful in your business.**

How you react to circumstances reveals your core beliefs. This course helps you identify the automatic triggers hindering your success and helps you master communication skills to respond effectively.

This book contains thoroughly road-tested, step-by-step skills and learning methods to make you more successful in your business. As you complete the activities you will develop a greater awareness of how to respond in ways that will repay you both personally and financially.

Insights about Core Beliefs:

You may or may not be aware of your core beliefs. Many core beliefs are *acted* out but not *thought* out.

Core beliefs are demonstrated not by what you say they are, but by your actions.

You can hold beliefs that you say you feel strongly about. However, if you do not *live them out*, they do not define who you really are.

"Consistent" does not mean that you live your core beliefs out perfectly; rather, it means the usual way you live. For example, you may have a core belief about the importance of exercising regularly. If you exercise regularly, but once in a while you miss exercising for a few days, then you are living that core belief. However, if you only exercise once every month or so, this is not one of your core beliefs; it is only a belief.

When a core belief accurately reflects truth and reality, it motivates you to act appropriately and effectively. Of course the opposite is also true. Some of your core beliefs may be false and lead you to act inappropriately and undermine your personal, career or business success.

Core beliefs are personal. Core beliefs are not something anyone can impose on you. When I share a core belief in this book, I am not demanding consensus.

Look at each core belief in this book, then:

- Wrestle with where you are in relation to the core belief.
- Consider if you believe it.
- Ask yourself if you act it out.
- Evaluate if you want it to be yours.
- Make it your core belief or determine what you want your core belief to be in the area presented.
- Modify your actions to reflect what you truly believe at your core.

Comfort Zone

Your comfort zone is comprised of your living, work, social, and communication experiences. This mental boundary makes you feel secure and comfortable, rather than anxious or threatened. However, these internal boundaries may result in ineffective communication skills.

Your comfort zone directly affects your dreams, goals and business success. In order to build winning business relationships, you have to identify what you are doing that is not working. Then learn new skills, which require moving to a new comfort zone. Once the new skills are automatic, your old comfort zone will be unacceptable.

The goal of this workbook is to push you beyond the edges of the communication comfort zones hindering your relationships. You can and should push beyond your fears and the security of your comfort zone. It is necessary for success.

The core beliefs in this book will help you think about pushing yourself towards the comfort zone that will be most beneficial for you, your career, your business, and all your relationships.

> **Your comfort zone directly affects your dreams, goals and business success.**

Small, Carefully Guarded Comfort Zone

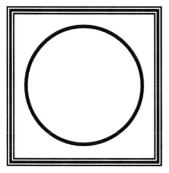

The thick circle on the left illustrates a small, carefully-guarded comfort zone. If you have a comfort zone like this, you will try to avoid anything that makes you feel uncomfortable. This type of comfort zone inhibits growth.

When you have a new opportunity, you will push it away, because it is uncomfortable.

Permeable Comfort Zone

The design on the right illustrates someone who has a permeable comfort zone. He allows uncomfortable experiences into his life. As a result, his circle is constantly changing as he grows to incorporate new experiences.

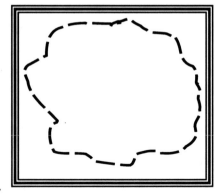

NOTE: You may have a combination of both types of comfort zones. For example, you may have areas of your life where you are not open to change, but have other areas where you are willing to grow.

Think about it:

1. Draw what you think your comfort zone looks like now.

2. What would you like your comfort zone to look like?

3. What might you need to change to be more successful in your business, career or personal relationships?

Four Stages to Build New Patterns

This book challenges you to examine how well you communicate. The core beliefs provide a new way of thinking to build successful business relationships. Like remodeling a house, the step-by-step learning process helps you identify the precise actions you need to incorporate, so you can be successful. As you complete the activities, you build your communication skills and learn how to respond. Below, you will find the building stages to learn a new skill.

Stage 1   *Awareness Stage:* You become aware of a new skill. For example you see the skill demonstrated or you read about it.

Stage 2   *Awkward Stage:* As you begin practicing the communication skill, it feels awkward. It doesn't feel like the natural way to respond. Some people become stuck at this stage. Since it immediately feels unnatural, some simply give up.

Stage 3   *Do It by the Numbers:* The skill no longer feels awkward. You can do the skill, but you still have to deliberately concentrate on how to perform it. Otherwise, you fall back into old patterns.

Stage 4   *Integration:* You find yourself automatically doing the skill. It is your core belief—a part of who you are.

How to Use this Course

There are many ways you can use this book, including:

Study it alone.

It is easy to let "more important" things crowd out time for study. To grow and maximize exceptional customer-service and people skills—

- Make a commitment to seriously study this book.

- Find someone to hold you accountable.

- Complete assignments to take full advantage of strengthening effective communication skills.

- Write your answers in a separate notebook or journal, if you need more room than this book has, or if you borrowed this from a library.

Study it with a small group.

I highly recommend interacting with others, as you will learn more. Read through the suggestions for small groups in "Appendix A: Small Groups." Each chapter has activities to complete.

Study with one other person.

Use the recommendations for small groups in "Appendix A: Small Groups."

Attend Success Builders International's Customer Service Communication Workshop.

You will gain the most from this book if you study it first, and then attend one of Success Builders International' practical and interactive workshops. To find a workshop near you or to schedule or sponsor a workshop, log on to www.SuccessBooks.info.

1

How to Avoid Sabotaging Your Profit$

Individuals who build the most successful relationships and businesses know how to communicate with others.

Individuals who cultivate the most successful personal and businesses know how to communicate with others. They are good listeners. For many, listening is far more difficult than talking. Are you thinking?

"I'm pretty good at hitting it off with others."

"I can carry my own in conversations."

"I know how to sabotage my relationships."

The secret to building long-lasting, two-way relationships involves more than a winning personality or charisma. The foundation of positive relationships is communication skills that allow you to focus on others.

- Do you desire to connect with your customers and coworkers? Most people desire to connect with others. Yet, they often fail to realize how they are creating distance between themselves and others.

- Many people are unaware of what they do that hurts or kills their relationships. As you study this chapter, you can identify how you create distance with others or connect to build rapport. Keep an open mind so you will discover what you may be doing (or not doing) that kills or maims your business relationships.

> **Companies that don't deliver exceptional customer service will be crowded out of the marketplace.**

Have you ever missed out on a sale because you did something to sabotage the relationship? Most salespeople can answer "yes" to that question. To ensure exceptional customer service this series provides training that will help avoid that mistake in the future.

Sabotaging Relationships is Natural for Many Salespeople

Answer these questions honestly:

- Are relationship saboteurs[1] natural for you?

- Have you ever wondered why you have *two ears* and only *one mouth*?

- Is it easier for you to talk than to listen?

- Do you define "communication" as "talking"? Talking is important, but the crucial component in building strong business relationships is skillful listening.

- Have you ever had a customer buy from another salesperson, when you were both offering the same deal?

- Could you be losing profits in your business because you do things you may not even be aware you're doing?

Many business writers and speakers talk about the importance of having good people skills. This course teaches how to practically improve these skills. Exceptional interpersonal skills are essential in every aspect of business but most especially in sales.

> **This book is designed to help you develop and improve the communication skills needed to be successful in your business.**

---

[1] See "Relationship Saboteurs Checklist" on page 38

An "I don't care" attitude is ravaging businesses from the assembly line to the retail floor. The Gallup Organization research and consulting firm estimates 70 percent of employees are "disengaged," meaning they are no longer committed to the company. Even worse, the longer employees stay, the more disengaged they become.

Communication can easily make or break your career or business success.

> ## Most businesses rate their customer service a 9 on a scale of 1 to 10, but their customers don't rate them near as high.

An Example of How to Sabotage a Relationship and Lose Huge Profits

Linda, a successful career woman, and her husband, Bill, went to look at a new car. When they approached Tom, the salesperson, Linda informed him the car was for her.

As Tom reviewed the car's features, he ignored Linda and directed all his comments and questions toward Bill. As they prepared to test drive the car, Tom assumed Bill would be the driver. Linda corrected Tom and got in the driver's seat. When Tom demonstrated the makeup mirror located on the passenger's side visor, Linda was insulted.

Even though she loved the car, Linda refused to purchase the car from Tom. They went to another dealership and purchased the same make and model—a $60,000 luxury car. They bought it from a salesperson who treated Linda with the same respect as her husband.

From Good to Great

Communication skills are essential for success. If you have poor customer-service communication skills, you may be able to service some customers. But is your goal to be successful in your job or just survive? With the same effort *and* good interpersonal skills, you can increase your success, income potential and business profits.

> **Your ability to communicate effectively increases your ability to become wealthy.**

Every person you encounter in your career or business has personal needs. Most will respond to someone who shows them concern. As you become more focused on others, you will find more people *want* to do business with you. Taking a few extra minutes to listen and find out the desires of your prospect or customer will reward you personally and financially.

Simply reading about building relationships with communication skills is not enough. To obtain exceptional customer-service and people skills, you must actively apply the principles and skills taught.

"Sometimes as leaders we create barriers for people to get work done, and we're unwilling to listen," says Theresa Welbourne, CEO of eePulse Inc., a technology and management research company in Michigan.

Businesses need to train every employee in customer-service communication—even those who don't have customer contact. You never know who the customer will have contact with—workers in sales, shipping, accounting, even product development. An exceptional service program cannot be limited to specific employees. It is everybody's job.

When it comes to customer service, actions speak louder than words. Using good communication skills, doesn't take extra money or time. However, dealing with dissatisfied customers and replacing lost customers does take an immense about of time and money.

> # A business
> ## —even one that can't afford extensive advertising—
> ## can still differentiate itself from competitors on the basis
> ## of exceptional customer service.

"Build two-way communication. When it comes to customer relations, 'listening' can be every bit as important as 'telling.' Use every tool and opportunity to create interaction. Customers who know they're 'heard' instantly feel a rapport and a relationship with your company," says Kim Gordon, author of *Bringing Home the Business* and one of the country's foremost experts on entrepreneurial success. (Kim Gordon, *7 Relationship-Building Strategies for Your Business;* January 05, 2004 http://www.entrepreneur.com/article/0,4621,312509,00.html.)

Salespeople Use Communication Skills with a Variety of People...

Your ability to communicate effectively increases your ability to become wealthy. Success in your business career includes establishing connections with:

Customers:

- People looking to buy immediately
- People thinking about buying at some point in the future
- People who know others who want to buy
- People who know others and will pass on your information

Coworkers:

- Other salespeople

- Agents

- Suppliers

- Contractors

- Referrals or affiliates who bring you deals

...and in Every Kind of Sale

- Straight sales

- Financed sales

- Wholesale

- Rentals

- Leasing

**There are hundreds of ways to lose customers.
The more competition you have in your marketplace,
the more you need to offer exceptional service.
If your customer service that isn't a top priority
it is probably bad customer service.**

Two Proven Techniques to Improve Communication Skills

You may have great knowledge about your business, customer service or sales. However, if you're unaware of what you're doing wrong, you can damage your relationships with others.

If you consistently communicate poorly with others, you will eventually hurt or kill your relationships as well as any business opportunities! If you use relationship saboteurs, you will loose customers, deals and profits.

This book is designed to help you develop and improve the communication skills needed for exceptional customer service.

The two ways to grow in interpersonal skills are:

1. Discover what you do that is *ineffective* and stop doing it, or at least do it less often. If you do not recognize how you hurt your relationships, how can you change?

2. Discover what is *more effective* and start doing it. Or, if you already practice the skill, perfect it. Do it better. Do it more often.

**You may have great knowledge about your business, customer service or sales.
However, if you're unaware of what you're doing wrong, you can damage your relationships with others.**

Reflect

How detrimental can it be *not* to listen? Consider your responses to the following questions:

1. Recall a time when you were hurting and desperately needed someone to understand your situation. You tried to talk with a friend or coworker, and realized he was not listening.

   a. How did his failure to listen and understand make you feel at that time?

   b. As you think back on it, how do you feel today?

   c. Did you ever go back to that person to share how he made you feel?

2. Have you ever failed to give your attention to a friend or coworker who needed someone to understand his circumstances? If so, how did it affect your relationship with that person?

A True-to-Life Story:
Relationship Building Pay$ Off

Scott, a successful salesperson for an assembly line machines manufacturer, receives a call from Paul, who owns a small company. Paul has been a customer of a competing company that has gone out of business. He wants to replace his current machine with a comparable model from Scott's company. He is ready to sign a contract as soon as Scott faxes it to him.

In addition to making a comparable model, Scott's company also manufactures newer models that can perform more operations. Scott decides to dig a little deeper. He asks Paul to tell him about his business. He listens intently and decides that a visit to Paul's premises might be beneficial. Although Paul is ready to sign, Scott gently suggests that if he can see Paul's business in action, he might find him a better machine.

It costs Scott's company over $2000 to send Scott out of state to visit Paul, but it pays off. After visiting for two days, Scott learns about the business and builds a relationship. Then he is able to customize products to Paul's way of doing business. He shows Paul how to automate a portion of his business that has never been automated.

Scott's recommendations will save Paul thousands of dollars in time and personnel. Paul buys a more expensive machine than he originally wanted to order. However, it will save money in the long run. And, Scott's company makes $100,000 more in profit by selling the higher end machine.

Was It Worth It?

- Scott spent about $2000 of his company's money and two days of his time to visit the customer in order to listen and learn about his business.

- He sold the customer a $500,000 machine rather than a $250,000 one, increasing his company's profits by $100,000.

- Scott made a long-term customer because he is the only sales representative who took the time to listen and learn about Paul's relatively small assembly business.

- Scott gained trust because he showed Paul how to automate more of his business.

Think About It:

- Would it be worth it for you to take the time to listen attentively to your customer's unique needs?

- What if listening and learning brought you a much larger sale or a larger commission?

- What if you made a long-term customer out of the deal?

- If you knew your commission would be directly affected, would it be worth the time to make your company an extra $100,000?

Relationship Saboteurs Checklist

Ways to Push People Away Without Really Trying

Which of the following relationship saboteurs have you used?

Nonverbal Relationship Saboteurs

- ☐ Don't return phone calls
- ☐ Don't listen
- ☐ Act sleepy or yawn
- ☐ Answer the phone and carry on another conversation
- ☐ Be reluctant to put reading material down
- ☐ Clean your fingernails
- ☐ Turn away from the speaker
- ☐ Give little eye contact; stare into space or look at other things or people
- ☐ Give too much eye contact; stare in the person's eyes without wavering
- ☐ Fold your arms
- ☐ Keep watching TV while the person talks
- ☐ Lean back in your chair and look at the ceiling or close your eyes
- ☐ Repeatedly look at your watch
- ☐ Answer your cell phone or send text messages
- ☐ Look bored, impatient, or upset with person
- ☐ Roll your eyes
- ☐ Fidget
- ☐ Play with pen or keys
- ☐ Remain seated while the other person stands

- ☐ Shake your head in disgust

- ☐ Show impatience by your tone of voice

- ☐ Shuffle papers on your desk

- ☐ Sit absolutely still, with no response

- ☐ Smile or wave at someone walking by or across the room

- ☐ Use inappropriate facial expressions; for example, smile when the other person is sad

Verbal Relationship Saboteurs

- ☐ Be more concerned about finishing the transaction rather than providing exceptional service

- ☐ Downplay a customer's hardships

- ☐ Don't give solid answers to a customer's questions

- ☐ Tell a customer one answer then change your mind later

- ☐ Ask lots of specific questions, but don't respond to the answers

- ☐ Belittle or condemn the person speaking or other people

- ☐ Belittle the problem:
    - o *It's not that expensive.*
    - o *It's not all that bad.*
    - o *What's the big deal?*

- ☐ Finish the person's sentences

- ☐ Give simplistic advice on what to do, think and feel:
    - o *If I were you I would...*
    - o *Our company's policy doesn't...*

- ☐ Interrupt often

☐ Change the subject

☐ Mind read:

- o *I know what you're thinking.*

- o *You're really angry. Admit it.*

- o *I know exactly how you feel.*

☐ Prophesy:

- o *If you don't buy this product or service, you'll never be able to find this kind of deal again.*

- o *The way you're going, you'll never be able to make a decision about what you want.*

☐ Put the person down for his feelings:

- o *You shouldn't feel that way.*

- o *That's stupid to feel sad.*

☐ Turn the subject to yourself and your problems or exciting stories

☐ Use loaded words:

- o *"blubbering"*

- o *"whining"*

- o *"having a pity party"*

☐ Other comments:

- o *Don't worry about it.*

- o *I resolved my problem; you ought to be able to resolve yours in the same way.*

- o *It's hopeless.*

- o *My problem is worse than yours.*

- o *You don't know what you're talking about.*

Review the Relationship Saboteurs You Have Used

1. Have you ever lost a deal because your relationship saboteurs hindered effective communication?

   a. If so, identify the relationship saboteurs you used.

   b. What was the result or impact of your behavior?

   c. What could you have done differently?

2. Have you ever used relationship saboteurs with a coworker or customer?

   a. If so, identify the relationship saboteurs you utilized.

   b. What was the result or impact of your behavior?

   c. What could you have done differently?

Core Beliefs about Relationships

Your core beliefs determine how you live your life. If you didn't read the "Core Beliefs Dramatically Affect Your Profits" section on page 21, please review it now. It will help you understand this section.

Summary: A core belief is *a firmly held conviction that consistently motivates my behavior.*

Belief + Consistent Action = Core Belief

Core Belief #1
One measure of my respect for others is how well I listen to them.

Think about Core Belief #1 and answer the following questions:

1. What does this core belief mean to you in your job, career or business?

2. How does listening respect others?

3. How do you react to Core Belief #1?

4. What could you change that will maximize your exceptional customer-service skills?

> ## Core Belief #2
> ### If I use relationship saboteurs with my customers and coworkers, my business will not be as successful.

Think about Core Belief #2 and answer the following questions:

1. What does this core belief mean to you in your job, career or business?

2. How could relationship saboteurs keep you from offering exceptional customer service?

3. How do you react to Core Belief #2?

4. What could you change to maximize customer-service effectiveness in your job, career or business?

> ## Core Belief #3
> ### I can hurt my relationships, without ever saying a word, through nonverbal communication.

Think about this Core Belief #3 and answer the following questions:

1. What does this core belief mean to you in your job, career or business?

2. How can nonverbal communication hurt your business?

3. How do you react to Core Belief #3?

4. What could you change to maximize your ability to provide exceptional customer service?

Nonverbal Communication Is Critical to Your Business Success

"If you think you will excel with technical skills alone; you are dead wrong!" writes Bill Twyford in *Secrets of Closing the Deal.*

Some of the most powerful communication tools are the ones most sales people are not aware of—the nonverbal aspects. Nonverbal communication speaks louder than words.

Understanding nonverbal communication is critical to your job, career or business. It is essential to build rapport and to negotiate with customers and coworkers. Once you establish rapport, barriers disappear and trust grows. Only then will customers choose to work with you, instead of working with another business or salesperson.

Nonverbal communication is a person's use of voice and body, rather than spoken words. It is all the messages, other than words, that a person uses in his relationships.

- *Voice* is how you say the words—vocal pitch, inflection or intonation, rate of speech, manner of speaking, and delivery.

- *Body language* is the unspoken communication that goes on in every face-to-face encounter with another person. It is how you use your body, eyes and face to communicate.

> **"Our nonverbal messages often contradict what we say in words. When we send mixed messages or our verbal messages don't jibe with our body statements, our credibility can crumble."**
> **Jo-Ann Vega, president of JV Career And Human Resources Consulting Services, Nyack, N.Y.**

Your nonverbal communication conveys subtle messages about your customer-service effectiveness. Your ability to positively affect their senses impacts your ability to sell.

Whenever there is a conflict between someone's words and their body signals and movements, we tend to believe their body.

Regardless of what type of product or service you sell, your communication skills, both verbal and nonverbal, determine whether you will provide exceptional customer service to obtain the sale.

Words are only a small part of our communication. Look at the chart on page 46. Ninety-three percent of how you communicate is not with your words. That's amazing! Simply learning the right words to say, doesn't ensure success in business.

Customer service is a people business—*everything you do involves people.* Most sales courses focus on the importance of the words we use, but fail to mention the importance of your body language and tone of voice. If you only focus on the words you use with your customers, you miss 93 percent of communication. Nonverbal communication can hurt your relationships with customers.

Communication

Body Language and Voice = 93%

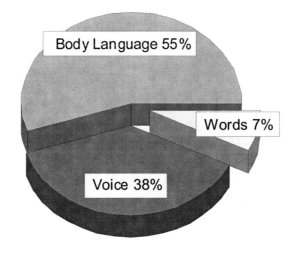

Body Language 55%

Voice 38%

Words 7%

- Body Language 55%
- Voice 38%
- Words 7%

**You are responsible for how your customers react.
Your words, tonalities, and body language
cause the communication from your customer.
If you don't like how your customers are responding
to you, change your body and tone.
This represents 93 percent of your communication.**
Bill Twyford, *The Secrets of Closing the Deal*
www.1234closures.com. 303-838-5532

Are You Aware of What You Communicate Nonverbally?

Learning to recognize what your customers and others say nonverbally gives you a competitive edge. Understanding your customer's nonverbal cues can mean the difference between success, failure and customer satisfaction.

Familiarizing yourself with basic nonverbal signals improves your ability to understand what people really communicate. Plus you become aware of what your nonverbal cues broadcast to the world.

Body Language Spells Relational and Monetary Success

Body language is a valuable tool to influence your customers and coworkers. There is no denying the link between effective nonverbal skills and success. Body language is the secret, quiet and most powerful language of all! People's bodies send out messages constantly, telling their true feelings towards you and how well your words are being received. How often do you fail to recognize what you or others communicate nonverbally?

Your ability to read and understand your clients' body language can mean the difference between making a great or poor impression.

> **Body language is the secret, quiet, and most powerful language of all.**

An important way to develop rapport with a client is to mirror his nonverbal cues. Match his body language and tone of voice. For example, if he talks fast, you talk fast; if he folds his arms, you fold yours. To learn more about the power of mirroring, contact Success Builders International.

You will damage or possibly kill your relationships if you are unaware of—

- What the other person conveys nonverbally

- What you communicate with nonverbal signals

Dishonest sales people will be exposed when customers read their body language like a book. Then these prospective customers will turn to you—the honest, customer-service professional—for their business solutions.

To be successful in customer service, you must be able to do the following:

- Recognize and improve the nonverbal signs you send to your customers.

- Identify your client's nonverbal signals and respond well to them.

- Build rapport with your customer by mirroring him.

Success Books has a 45-page booklet about nonverbal communication. Please go to www.SuccessBooks.info to request the e-book.

What Would I Do to Increase My Profit$?

Read each story. Then answer the questions.

1. John, a mobile-phone salesman, works for a profitable retail mobile-phone store. After a rough month, John has only two days left to make his monthly quota. Susan walks into the store—obviously distressed. She is a new business owner and a current customer. Susan accidentally ran over her mobile phone and doesn't have insurance. She has to replace the unit at her own expense.

   John is annoyed. The commission on selling a phone to a current customer is much less than selling a phone/service combination. He doesn't want to waste his time on this customer. Susan is concerned about the cost of replacing the phone, even though she knows it is necessary to her business. John wants her to pick a phone quickly so he can wait on other customers. Susan wants to vent her frustration about breaking a phone she can't afford to replace.

   a. How would you normally respond to this situation?

   b. What relationship saboteurs might you be tempted to use?

   c. What do you think the best way(s) would be to respond to this situation?

   d. How can you prepare yourself to handle a situation like this?

   e. If you respond to Susan with relationship saboteurs, how will this hurt your job, career or business?

   f. Have you ever been in a situation like this? If so, what was the result? What could you have done differently?

2. Tammy is a telemarketing professional who sells vacations. To make her monthly quota, she must sell at least three more vacations tonight. She calls Denise. Before she begins her pitch about the great Bahamas deal, Denise bursts into tears. Tammy is tempted to hang up. She feels compelled to talk to the woman, though she is too busy to spend time with anyone unlikely to buy. Denise tells Tammy how she saved to take a big vacation, but now her child's illness is costing so much money. She fears she'll never be able to take her son on a vacation, even though she longs to take him to Disneyland. Tammy's business instincts tell her this conversation is probably a waste of time.

    a. How would you normally respond in a situation like this? What relationship saboteurs might you be tempted to use? Or what saboteurs has someone used on you in a similar situation?

    b. What do you think the best way(s) would be to respond to this situation?

    c. What might you need to do to prepare yourself to handle a situation like this?

    d. If you respond with relationship saboteurs, how could this hurt your ability to make a sale, obtain a referral or return business?

    e. Have you ever had a situation like this? If so, what was the result? What could you have done differently?

3. Carlos, a car salesman, specializes in high-end luxury cars. Mark walks in ready to purchase an expensive Porsche—with cash. Carlos is obviously excited, as this will be his biggest sale of the quarter. Since Mark doesn't need financing, Carlos rushes to process this "slam-dunk" sale.

   However, as they're completing the paperwork, Mark starts to tell Carlos details about his recent, ugly divorce. His wife was unfaithful. He just turned 40. And, he wants this car desperately, even though he realizes that it's the stereotypical, midlife-crisis vehicle. Fearing Mark might back out, Carlos hurries to complete the transaction. Mark, however, wants to keep discussing how his life has changed. The more Mark talks, the more Carlos sees the sale possibly disintegrating.

   a. How would you normally respond to this situation?

   b. What relationship saboteurs might you be tempted to use? Or what saboteurs have been used on you in a similar situation?

   c. What do you think the best way(s) would be to respond to this situation?

   d. What might you need to do to prepare yourself to handle a situation like this?

   e. If you respond with relationship saboteurs, how could this hurt your potential for referrals and return business?

   f. Have you ever faced a situation similar to this? If so, what was the result? What could you have done differently to provide exceptional customer service?

How Am I at Sabotaging My Relationships?

Consider your relationships with coworkers and customers.
Use this scale to indicate your responses.
You may use a separate sheet to write your answers.

1 = Hardly ever
2 = Occasionally
3 = Sometimes
4 = Often
5 = Nearly always

Clients Coworkers

____   ____   1.   I often interrupt others and/or finish their sentences.

____   ____   2.   I fidget, move around a lot, and do things with my hands while others talk to me.

____   ____   3.   If someone says something that triggers a thought or idea, I say it immediately.

____   ____   4.   I interject my story and play "mine's better than yours" or "mine's worse than yours."

____   ____   5.   I am distracted by others around me when a person talks to me about important matters.

____   ____   6.   I am quick to give advice whenever I believe I have the answer to people's problems.

_____ _____ 7. I look at my watch often when the other person is talking.

_____ _____ 8. If I think someone has a major problem, I do not hesitate to tell them.

_____ _____ 9. If I am feeling impatient, bored, or upset with the person, I show it however I can.

_____ _____ 10. I tell people how I solved my problems, so they can know how to solve theirs.

_____ _____ 11. I ask many questions rather than listening to what the person says.

_____ _____ 12. If what the person says triggers something that interests me, I quickly change the subject so I can talk about my interest.

_____ _____ 13. I tend to discern people's motives and thoughts. I do not hesitate to tell them what I believe they think and why they act the way they do.

_____ _____ 14. I "help" people with their problems by letting them know their situation is not all that bad and things always get better.

Look over your responses to *How Am I at Sabotaging My Relationships?*

1. **Congratulate yourself!** Did you score a 1 or a 2 in any of the situations? You are doing great!

2. **Needs Improvement.** Did you score a 3? Once you have improved the 4's and 5's, work on the 3's. If you scored a 4 or 5 come up with an action plan to improve each area of concern. Then choose one or two issues to begin working on right now. Which one will you start with?

3. Talk with someone who will hold you accountable. Who will you talk to?

Opportunities for Growth

Note: Choose the opportunities below that you believe will be most profitable for you. Choose one or two areas to start on, because trying to change in too many areas at one time can be overwhelming.

1. Review the "Relationship Saboteurs Checklist" on page 38.

    a. List the relationship saboteurs you tend to use most often.

    b. With whom have you used them most frequently, and/or most destructively?

    c. What has been the result?

2. Family members, close friends or business associates can be a great asset to you. They provide the best feedback to help you recognize relationship saboteurs that can damage your relationships and business. Give one or two of them the "Relationship Saboteurs Checklist" and ask them to check behaviors that you have done with them. Then ask them the following questions:

    a. What behaviors do I have that make it difficult for you to talk openly with me?

    b. How would you like me to change in this area?

3. Using the "Relationship Saboteurs Checklist," discuss the following with a family member, good friend, or a coworker.

    a. The relationship saboteurs I realize that I sometimes use with you are…

    b. Which relationship saboteurs are you aware of that I use with you?

c. What relationship saboteurs do you see me using with others?

d. Are we willing to admit immediately these relationship saboteurs to each other when we realize that we've used them? If so, when will we begin?

e. Invite him to gently remind you when he sees you use a relationship killer with him, customers or coworkers. Discuss how best he can tell you and when.

4. What relationship saboteurs do I tend to use with each of the following?

a. Potential customers

b. Return customers

c. Customers who come with a problem with my product or service.

d. Coworkers

5. After talking with your family, friends or business associates and evaluating the verbal and nonverbal behaviors that kill your relationships, list what you plan to do to improve your communication skills.

6. Practice Makes Profit$: An important part of learning the skills in this book is to practice them. There is a DVD that goes along with this book. Each skill is demonstrated on the training DVD. For this chapter, you will watch, *How to Avoid $abotaging Your Profit$*. It demonstrates ways people may sabotage their relationships without even know it. The DVD includes instructions for how to benefit from watching it. If you don't have a copy of the DVD, you can get one at www.SuccessBooks.Info.

7. Turn to the last pages of this book, entitled "Snapshots." Write down one or two things you want to remember or work on from this chapter. Or you can make a new page in your journal for these entries. You'll write something after each chapter that you want to remember.

2

Maximize Profit$: How to Listen to Provide Exceptional Customer Service

"Eighty-five percent of one's financial success can be attributed to people skills and only fifteen percent from technical skills"
—The Carnegie Institute of Technology

What Is the Most Important Communication Skill You Can Incorporate Into Your Customer Service?

Listen.   Be quiet.   **Listen.**   Don't Talk.

Don't interrupt.   **Listen.**   Shushhh.   **Listen.**

Listen.   Keep quiet.   **Listen.**   Pay attention.

Keep Silent.   **Listen.**   Don't Speak.   **Listen.**

Listen.   Ignore the phone.   **Listen.**   Hush.

Act interested.   **Listen.**   Be attentive.   **Listen.**

Listen.   Stay silent.   **Listen.**   Take note.

Remain silent.   **Listen.**   Don't Talk.   **Listen.**

Listen.   Don't Talk.   **Listen.**   Don't interrupt.

Active listening is one of the best ways to build rapport and trust to increase sales. People treat listening as a last-resort strategy. If all else fails, listen.

One of the primary factors to give exceptional service is to *listen carefully*. Pay attention to what the customer wants, rather than being preoccupied with your work. Show courtesy to every customer—whether in person, on the phone or by mail.

> **"You can never go too far
> in providing customer service.
> You have to get into the mindset
> of your customers.
> You have to ask them questions,
> listen to them and follow up with them."**
> **says Brad Sobel, CEO and co-founder of eHobbies**

The quickest, least expensive way to retain customers and increase profits is to be a customer-service leader.

What is the super glue that cements the deal when you work with customers who complain? Listening is the bonding agent to build dynamic relationships in business, as well as relationships in families, friendships, the work environment, and in the community.

All sales people and customer-service professionals meet individuals who need someone to understand their situation. Many potential customers with problems particularly need a kind, nonjudgmental ear. Listening without judging or giving advice is the best technique to pave the way to seal the deal.

Developing the skill of active listening can increase your profits exponentially. The more you learn to listen, the more people will want to:

- Buy your product

- Send you referrals

- Purchase from you a second time

If you want to build financially winning relationships, you need to actively listen to:

Coworkers, who include:

- business partners
- other sales people
- contractors who install or service your product
- other business professionals

> # Listening is the highest form of courtesy.
> ### Bill Twyford, *The Secrets of Closing the Deal*

Customers, including:

- Potential customers

- Return customers who are ready to buy again

- Customers who have a problem with your product or service

Your family and friends. This book does not focus on personal relationships. However, good interpersonal skills usually begin in your closest interactions. Practicing these skills in your personal relationships will make it easier to use them in business situations.

Have you ever noticed that we have eyelids that close and mouths that shut, but no *ear lids*? Did you ever wonder why we can't close our ears?

The skill of respectful listening is foundational to all relationships, yet few people do it well. Your customer-service skills will stand above the crowd when you develop this critical skill.

> **Your customer-service skills**
> **will stand above the crowd**
> **when you develop this critical skill—**
> **listening with respect.**

Seven Principles of Listening

If you want to develop exceptional customer-service skills, apply these principles to all your interactions. Using these skills effectively will build rapport and give you the edge you need in negotiating.

1. **Communicate your willingness to listen and to help the person.** Ask yourself:

   a. Does your body language reveal that you will take the time to listen?

   b. Have you communicated that you are available to listen with your attention and your words?

   c. Are you able to withhold advice or critical comments?

   d. Are you focused on understanding what the person is saying and feeling rather than on what you want to say?

> **Using these skills effectively will build rapport and give you the edge you need in negotiating.**

2. **Determine on what level the person is communicating by what he is saying.** Then respond on the same level. Review the "Where Are You?" illustration on the next page.

    a. When someone talks to you, the first question to ask yourself is, "What level is this person on: head or heart?"

    b. Then respond on the same level. If you don't respond on the same level, you will not connect.

    c. However, when a person is on _both_ head and heart levels, you can decide on which you will respond first.

Sometimes people cross levels. For example, imagine a customer is telling you that he needs to buy new furniture because his home burned down, and he must now furnish his apartment. He tells you how difficult this has been for him, you interrupt to ask him, "Are you interested in leather or fabric?" How do you think that would make him feel? Are you communicating that you are interested in _him_, or are you conveying that your only interest in him is in making money off his devastating circumstances?

When someone begins talking with you, ask yourself:

    a. _Is he on the head level?_ Is the customer reporting facts, ideas, or thoughts? Respond on a head level with your ideas, facts, advice, solutions, and opinions.

    b. _Is he on the heart level?_ Is the customer sharing feelings—either painful or happy experiences? Listen carefully. Be considerate. Try to understand with your heart what is being disclosed to you. Show empathy and understanding.

Work at understanding your customer and relating on his level, even when you might prefer to communicate on another level. An ancient proverb says, "A fool finds no pleasure in understanding, but delights in airing his opinions."

WHERE ARE YOU?

HEAD LEVEL

HEART LEVEL

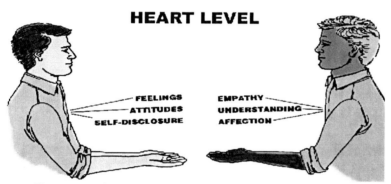

Respond on the same conversational level

To be effective in your communication, stay on the same level as the person who is sharing. If he is on a heart level, he needs your understanding. He does not need factual information or advice regarding how your service is better than your competitors.

On the other hand, if he is on the head level, he probably is not looking for empathy. For example, if the customer tells you matter-of-factly he needs to buy furniture to furnish his entire apartment. He's ready to buy now and wants the furniture delivered next week. He just wants to move on and get his life back to normal. If you say, "You must be really upset. Would you like to talk about what happened?" he may get angry and walk away. If you try to empathize with him when he is on the head level, you may lose the sale.

> **"You should listen twice as much as you talk.**
> **All you have to do is shut up and listen and watch people.**
> **You will be amazed at all you will learn."**
> **Bill Bronchick, Author, Speaker,**
> **Attorney & Best-Selling Author, Host of Legalwiz.com**

3. **Embrace the customer's feelings.** When a customer talks on a heart or emotional level, he wants his feelings, attitudes and self-disclosure to be heard. This opens the door to gain his trust and is an excellent way to build rapport.

   a. Can you imagine how the person feels?

   b. Can you put yourself in his place?

   c. Are you directing your thoughts toward his feelings and away from the urge to judge, condemn or disagree with him?

4. **Put your understanding of what the customer says into your words.** This is the most difficult step for most people.

   a. Do you understand what the person is feeling?

   b. Can you accept the validity of the other person's feelings?

   c. Expressing another person's feelings in your words lets the customer hear his feelings verbalized. It is not parroting, interpreting or approving of wrongdoing. It is simply stating what you heard him say.

5. **Ensure the customer is comfortable sharing what he feels.** Ask yourself:

   a. Have you responded in such a way that the person feels safe and encouraged to share more, but not pressured?

   b. Are you listening carefully to his words and observing his body language?

   c. Do you avoid pushing the customer to share more than he is comfortable to divulge?

   d. Do your questions or comments invite the person share more on a deeper level?

   e. Are you letting the other person lead the conversation, or are you leading the conversation with too many questions?

   f. Do you respect and allow the customer to stop talking when he does not want to continue communicating his feelings?

> **"Nothing I say will teach me anything. If I'm going to learn something, I'll have to do it by listening."**
> **Larry King, TV show host**
> **Get Motivated Seminar Workbook**

Observations, sensitive self-disclosure and a few well-placed questions make it easier for the person to share what is on his heart. The next chapter will detail each of these areas.

6. **Be sensitive for the right timing before trying to close the deal.** When a potential customer calls, it is tempting to go straight to closing the deal. Yet, before the customer is ready to commit to the sale, he may need to talk through some of his issues. If you listen to his issues with empathy, you may help develop the trust he needs before he purchases your products or services.

> ## You must know the person's heartfelt needs before you can address them. This takes time.

In an effort to get a customer to purchase your products or services, resolve a complaint or to influence a coworker to change in any way avoid these common mistakes:

a. Offering advice too quickly, without listening.

b. Providing solutions before hearing the complaint.

c. Jumping in too soon to show the customer how to resolve the situation.

d. Confronting the customer before you understand the whole picture of his problem.

You must know the person's heartfelt needs before you can address them. This takes time.

7. **Find out how people of other cultures build relationships.** Even though you may live in the United States (or any other country), remember that your country is filled with people from various cultures. To build exceptional customer-service relationships, communicate on the same level as your customer or coworker.

Cultural Relevance

Body language, gestures, personal space,
and the way people verbally express themselves
vary from region to region.
Many North Americans believe
the most important way to communicate is verbally.
However, most other cultures judge what you say
by your gestures, posture, and facial expressions.
Some cultures are more enthusiastic and expressive.
Others are more restrained.
Watch the customer's body language
and the way he expresses himself
to provide clues as to how you can appropriately respond.

A Final Thought

Unlocking someone's heartfelt emotions takes time. It is a fragile trust that can be easily shattered, destroying the potential to do business with that person. To build rapport—

- Replace judgmental critiques and advice with understanding, listening and encouraging affirmations.

- Resist the temptation to push your customers to reveal details you need before they are ready.

By simply taking the time to listen with caring and respect, you will be amazed at how customers will respond to your exceptional customer service. When you build customer rapport and serve their needs, they want to buy your products or services.

What can you learn from this axiom?
"He who answers before listening—
that is his folly and his shame."

A True-to-Life Story:
Active Listening Increases Profit$

Amy is a successful salesperson at a high-end furniture company. Joe and Trudy come into her store to buy a new bedroom suite. As they shop, they tell Amy they are renovating their house in stages. Right now, they are painting and refurnishing their master bedroom. In the next six to eight months, they plan to remove a wall between their attached master bath and a small adjacent bedroom to create a sitting room.

Genuinely interested in their renovation, Amy listens and asks pertinent questions. She points them to several bedroom collections with coordinating living-room furniture. Joe and Trudy purchase a set for $5000. Eight months later, they return to Amy. They spend another $5000 for the matching loveseat, coffee table and chairs to decorate their new master sitting room.

The Bottom Line:
- Because Amy listened, she pointed Joe and Trudy to bedroom furniture that coordinated with living-room furniture they can use later. They are happy with Amy's idea to think ahead regarding their renovation.

- When their renovation is complete, they return to the store and spend another $5000. Amy doubles her sale and her commission, because she took the time to listen.

Think About It:
- Amy doubles her commission. Was that worth taking the extra time to ask pertinent questions?

- If you were the manager or owner of the furniture company, would it have been worth the time and expense to train Amy to listen effectively?

- Is it worth taking a little extra time to listen and be courteous to a customer for an additional $5000 sale?

- What are you willing to do to double the sale of your product or service?

Core Beliefs about Listening

Your core beliefs determine how you live your life. If you didn't read the "Core Beliefs Dramatically Affect Your Profits" section on page 21, please review it now. It will help you understand this section.

Summary: A core belief is *a firmly held conviction that consistently motivates my behavior.*

Belief + Consistent Action = Core Belief

Core Belief #1
One measure of my respect of others is how well I listen to them.

There are many other ways to show respect, but attentive listening is one of the best.

Think about Core Belief #1 and answer the following questions:

1. How can listening develop exceptional customer service?

2. When someone shares his story, how do you normally act?

3. If you are tempted to move to the bottom line without listening to the customer, can you afford to continue acting this way? Why or why not?

4. What could you change that will help you be more successful in your job, career, business, or customer-service skills?

Core Belief #2
Listening is foundational to helping others.

Listening is absolutely essential in almost every part of your life.

Think about Core Belief #2 and answer the following questions:

1. Do you believe this? Give an example from your customer-service experiences.

2. Do you normally act as if listening is foundation to your business?

3. If not, how do you generally interact?

4. What could you change that will help you be more successful in your job, career, business, or customer-service skills?

Core Belief #3
Listening with respect is hard work.

To respect others by listening well requires effort, concentration and giving of yourself.

Think about Core Belief #3, then answer the following questions:

1. What do you think about core belief #1?

2. Is listening worth the hard work? Why or why not?

How to Listen Checklist

Here are a few specific skills and behaviors to keep in mind when dealing with customers or coworkers. Use this as a checklist to determine how you listen and what you want to improve.

Check the listening skills you most frequently use.

Nonverbal Listening Skills

☐ Set aside distractions quickly (TV, computer, newspaper)

☐ Ignore distractions around you (other people, noises)

☐ If needed, move to more private place

☐ Give focused attention

☐ Maintain appropriate eye contact

☐ Guard your tone of voice

☐ Use appropriate posture and facial expressions

☐ Turn your body toward the person (open posture)

☐ Keep your legs and arms uncrossed

☐ Touch as appropriate

☐ Be willing to take the time necessary to really listen

☐ Maintain a friendly distance

☐ Sit or stand on the same level

☐ If appropriate, invite the person to sit down

☐   Stay alert, awake and engaged

☐   Use culturally fitting responses to indicate interest, such as "hmmmmmmm"

☐   Nod your head

Verbal Listening Skills

☐   Give an invitation to talk

☐   Draw the person out with (these will be talked about more in the next chapter):

    o   silence

    o   open-ended questions

    o   self-disclosure

    o   observations

☐   Focus on the person's complaints or issues

☐   Stay on the subject at hand

☐   Bite your tongue! (Do not talk when you need to be listening quietly)

☐   Respond empathetically

☐   Give appropriate affirmations

☐   Ask few questions

☐   Allow the speaker to finish statements

☐   Respond on an appropriate head or heart level

☐   Acknowledge and validate his feelings

☐   Be encouraging

☐   Restate what you heard the person say to clarify understanding

Review the listening skills you most frequently use.

1. Which listening skills are you using most effectively to provide exceptional customer service?

2. Which listening skills would you like to begin using in your interactions?

3. Specifically, what will you do to incorporate new listening skills?

What Would I Do to Listen Effectively?

Look at the following true-to-life stories. Then answer the questions following them.

1. Adam is a sales associate at an electronics store. A mother, followed by two children, comes in to purchase an MP3 player. She knows exactly which brand and model she wants. She is anxious to purchase the product quickly and get on with her day. She has obviously done her research. Her choice is an excellent product—though not the most expensive MP3 player. Adam wants to show her other MP3 players and how a more expensive model would give her more features. Of course, he will receive a higher commission on the more expensive model, which is part of his motive. However, this lady is clearly on a mission. She knows exactly what she wants.

   a. How would you normally respond to this situation?

   b. What have you learned from this chapter that could help you provide exceptional customer service? Look at the "How to Listen Checklist" on page 72. Which of those skills could you implement in this situation?

   c. What might you need to do to prepare yourself to handle a similar situation?

   d. What do you think the outcome will be if Adam responds to the busy mother by trying to up sell her?

   e. How might the outcome be different if Adam responds by recognizing her rush, complimenting her on her research and quickly finishing the paperwork?

   f. Have you ever experienced a similar situation? If so, what was the result?

2. Jan, a computer salesperson, works with a customer who needs to buy a computer. Bill is somewhat strapped for cash, but wants a specific high-end brand because of its reliability record. Talk soon turns to money. He wants to share his current financial situation, so he doesn't run into trouble with financing. Bill says, "I recently started my own business and money is tight."

By listening, Jan discovers how much Bill can afford for a monthly payment. However, Jan realizes Bill will likely get turned down for financing on the model he prefers. This store offers a good price on a slightly less popular brand. The brand is also very reliable. It performs all of the functions Bill needs. Best of all, the monthly payments are ones he can afford.

a. What would your first thought be when you heard he was strapped for cash but wants a high-end computer? How you might be inclined to answer?

b. What have you learned from this chapter that could help you provide exceptional customer service? Look at the "How to Listen Checklist" on page 72. Which of those could you implement in this situation?

c. What might you need to do to prepare yourself to handle a situation like this?

d. What do you think the outcome will be if Jan gruffly responds, "Thank you for your time, but the computer you want costs more than you can afford?"

e. What do you think the outcome might be if Jan took the time to listen to him?

f. Have you ever had a situation like this? If so, what was the result?

3. Alex is a customer-service representative for a large cable television company. Maria calls to complain that her cable box is not functioning properly. The cable goes off and on. As Maria describes the situation, Alex is certain Maria's cable box has loose plugs and just needs to be properly plugged in. Maria tells Alex she checked all the connections multiple times. Alex feels annoyed. He is positive Maria doesn't know how to connect her box properly. He listens as she describes the trouble she's had and how everyone dismissed her. Everyone she called told her that her box is incorrectly connected. Though Alex is hesitant, he schedules a service call. When the technician arrives, he finds that Maria's box is indeed connected properly. He finds one of the cables has been partially chewed by an animal.

a. How would you normally respond to this situation?

b. What have you learned from this chapter that could help you respond better? Look at the "How to Listen Checklist" on page 72. Which of those could you implement in this situation?

c. What might you need to do to prepare yourself to handle a situation like this?

d. What do you think the outcome would be if Alex responded harshly to this frustrated customer, thinking simply that she just doesn't know how to plug in a box?

e. What do you think the outcome will be if Alex responds by slowing down to take time to listen to Maria to explore other possibilities for her problems?

f. Have you ever experienced a similar situation this? If so, what was the result?

How Am I at Listening?

Consider how you are at listening to clients and coworkers.
Use this scale to indicate your responses.
You may use a separate sheet to write your answers.

1 = Hardly ever
2 = Occasionally
3 = Sometimes
4 = Often
5 = Nearly always

Clients Coworkers

____ ____ 1. I am patient with those who have difficulty putting frustrations or concerns into words.

____ ____ 2. When someone wants to talk with me, I make sure he is physically comfortable.

____ ____ 3. I am concerned and empathetic when someone expresses deep feelings.

____ ____ 4. If I need uninterrupted time, I do whatever I can to get alone so I do not have to tell people not to bother me. For example, I may choose not to answer the phone when I'm not prepared to listen to anyone.

____ ____ 5. When someone talks with me, I encourage him to continue as long as he needs to, without changing the subject.

____ ____ 6. I give appropriate eye contact. I look at the person enough, but not too much.

_____ _____ 7. I withhold making judgments until I've heard the whole story.

_____ _____ 8. I hold in strict confidence what I am told, unless I have permission to tell others.

_____ _____ 9. I respect others' privacy by encouraging them—without force or manipulation—to talk from the heart.

_____ _____ 10. My body posture and other nonverbal behavior communicate interest in the person.

_____ _____ 11. My facial expression reflects that I am empathizing with the person.

_____ _____ 12. I try to learn and to apply culturally relevant listening techniques when meeting with customers from different cultures.

_____ _____ 13. If someone comes to talk about a serious matter, I let him know immediately if my time is limited by another commitment.

_____ _____ 14. When I am listening I keep interruptions, such as telephone calls, to a minimum. For example, I turn my phone off when I'm listening actively to a customer. If I'm on the phone with him, I don't put him on hold to get another call.

_____ _____ 15. I gladly stop what I am doing when someone comes to talk with me.

Look over your responses to *How Am I at Listening?*

1. **Congratulate yourself!** Did you score a 1 or a 2 in any of the situations? You are doing great!

2. **Needs Improvement.** Did you score a 3? Once you have improved the 4's and 5's, work on the 3's. If you scored a 4 or 5—

   a. Come up with an action plan to improve each area of concern.

   b. Choose one or two issues to begin working on right now. Which will one you start with?

3. **Talk with someone who will hold you accountable.**

   a. Who will you talk to?

   b. When will you call?

Opportunities for Growth

Note: Choose the opportunities below that you believe will be most profitable for you. Choose one or two to start on, because trying to change in too many areas at once can be overwhelming.

1. Look for opportunities to build relationships with customers and coworkers.

   a. Observe signs that indicate when someone wants to talk from the heart.

   b. List times when a customer or coworker may want to talk from the heart.

   c. How can you consciously practice your best listening skills?

2. Deliberately set aside time each day or each week to invite those closest to you to talk with you from the heart. The more you practice this skill the easier it becomes.

3. To practice, call a friend or coworker. Begin by saying something like, "I just wanted to know how things are going with you. Is this a good time to talk?"

4. Discuss your responses to "How Am I at Listening?" on page 78 with a coworker or friend.

   a. Talk about one area in which you would like to grow.

   b. Rate each other and discuss your perceptions of each other's listening skills.

   c. Ask: *In which areas do you think I am doing well?*

   d. Ask: *In which areas do you think I need to grow?*

5. Become accountable to each other for the areas in which you decide improvement is needed. Ask for feedback when you do well, and when you don't.

6. You can grow in building your relationships by asking a family member, a friend or coworker:

   a. *When you share with me from your heart, what do I do to help you?*

   b. *What would you like me to do differently when you share from your heart?*

7. What can you do differently to listen more attentively to customers who complain, feel frustrated or struggle with emotionally difficult issues?

8. Practice Makes Profit$: Practicing listening is very important. It will help you get better at so that your profits increase. I'm amazed at how many people think they are good listeners, yet are actually miserable failures in that area. If you don't have the DVD that goes along with this book, you can get it at www.SuccessBooks.info. It provides demonstrations of each skill and comes with a guide to show you how to gain the most from watching the DVD and then how to practice the skill in the most effective ways.

9. Turn to the last pages of this book entitled "Snapshots." Write down one or two things you want to work on from this chapter, either on those pages or in a separate journal.

3

How to Establish Rapport to Build Customer Loyalty

"The purposes of a man's heart
are deep waters,
but a man of understanding
draws them out."
—an ancient proverb

Imagine you are Sherlock Holmes searching for clues to solve a mystery. In your case, you are searching for "money clues. People leave verbal and nonverbal money clues revealing important hidden motivations. These clues are a direct line to establish customer satisfaction.

> ## People leave verbal and nonverbal money clues revealing hidden motivations.

A person's clues, whether conscious or unconscious, indicate he has an important issue or experience he wants to communicate. People leave signs to see if anyone will spot them and show an interest.

If we sincerely want to provide exceptional customer service to customers, employees and vendors, we must learn to recognize and respond well to money clues.

Many times customers or coworkers send clues hoping that someone will care enough to listen. When you take the time to understand the person's situation, you will be amazed at what you uncover. As you learn to draw out people's true needs, you will leave a positive, lasting impression, plus profits will soar.

Exceptional customer service involves more than simply being courteous. Two of the most powerful interpersonal skills you can develop to be the best with every customer, are:

1. Recognize people's clues.

2. Know how to *respond* to clues with concern, so the person wants to share his inner thoughts, feelings and desires.

Customer-focused attitudes recognize and respond to clues. Customers will open up to you and feel valued rather than used. They will tell you everything you need to know to structure customer service that works for them.

You will also build rapport and trust with your customers and prospects when they see that you care about them and their needs—not just about making money from them.

> ## Money Clues are...
> - **Freely given**
> - **Often tentative**
> - **Keys to the heart**
> - **Emotionally laden**
> - **Invitations to listen**
> - **Cries for help at times**
> - **Verbal and/or nonverbal**
> - **A need for someone to care**

Money Clues are...

1. **Freely given**—They are not elicited. They are natural and often unconscious.

2. **Verbal and/or nonverbal**—They can be either what someone says or does. Look in the "Nonverbal Money Clues List" and the "Verbal Money Clues List" following this section for examples of each.

3. **Keys to the heart**—They reveal what a customer or coworker thinks and feels.

4. **Emotionally laden**—Never head-level, they always have to do with a person's emotions. Even though the emotions may not appear to be obvious, they lie just below the surface.

5. **Invitations to listen**—Clues are an attempt to get someone to listen to feelings and what is going on in the person's heart.

6. **Often tentative**—Many times a person leaves a clue just to see if anyone will listen.

7. **Indicate a need for someone to care**—Often a customer looks for someone to show interest in his situation. Watch for little signs that he wants your concern.

8. **Cries for help at times**—Sometimes a customer has a severe problem he needs to talk about. However, he doesn't overtly bring it up. So he leaves clues about his problem.

Two of the most powerful interpersonal skills you can develop are:
1.   **recognize people's clues**
2.   **know how to empathetically respond their clues**

Nonverbal Money Clues List

A few examples of nonverbal clues include:

- Crying
- Silence
- Sighing
- Surprise
- Laughing
- Happiness
- Impatience

- Nervousness
- Tone of voice
- Defensiveness
- Body language
- Disappointment
- Avoiding eye contact
- Hostility or excitement
- Facial expressions, such as a grimace or a smile

Verbal Money Clues List

The possibilities for verbal clues are endless. Common examples include:

- Changing the subject
- Statements that express emotions
- Regurgitating issues or references to the same events
- Rhetorical questions:

  Who cares, anyway?

  Why would anyone be interested in me?

  Would you believe what just happened to me?

Manipulation and pressure crush clues, hiding a person's feelings. An individual who responds well to clues provide an invitation to another person to express his frustrations.

> **Manipulation and pressure crush clues hiding a person's feelings.**

Gain a Competitive Edge with Money Clues

Giving customers or coworkers your full attention makes them feel valued. Discovering how to recognize verbal and nonverbal clues—the direct link to customer satisfaction—gives you a competitive edge. To provide exceptional customer service—

- Focus on inviting customers or coworkers to talk

- Set aside your agenda

- Provide opportunities for others to talk about their concerns in a way that is most comfortable for them to communicate

Sometimes customers—

- are experiencing some kind of loss

- are stressed about finances

- have trouble deciding which product or service to purchase

- have unrelated problems

If you tune into their clues, you often discover which issues impact their decision making. Then you can focus on the concern as a caring person and a customer-service professional.

> **Learn to recognize and respond to clues.**
> **The benefits to your business will be immense.**

Responding to money clues

- builds rapport

- creates relationships

- provides customer service that is above and beyond what is expected

If you are a manager or employer, it is important to let employees communicate what is on their minds, especially in an economic slump. When the economy is unsettled people are more afraid to speak honestly, especially concerning bad news about the company. They fear that expressing their feelings or viewpoints may negatively effect their employment.

Yet, employers need to hear what their employees think and say. This skill of unlocking the doors to communication is essential for anyone in business, whether working with employees, coworkers or customers. Happy employees equal happy customers.

Customers who feel that they have been heard are much more likely to return with their business. If you show you care, they will be devoted to your company. One of the best ways to show you care is to listen and draw them out.

A phrase that will make your customers happy—"How can I help?" Then be quiet and listen to what they have to say. Customers want the opportunity to explain what they want and need. Too often, businesses guess what their customers need rather than listen to what they say their needs are.

By asking how you can help, you begin a dialogue. You are 'helping,' not 'selling.' Open-ended questions invite discussion.

> **One of the best things a business can do to meet needs is to** *really listen to the customer* **and find out what he needs and wants.**

People want customer-service representatives to be interested in them. When you recognize clues and respond appropriately to draw customers out, they will do business with you and send others your way. Very few people even recognize clues, much less know how to respond.

If you take the time to learn this skill, your business will skyrocket. This skill takes time and effort to master, but it is well worth it.

Focus Your Responses

When you see or hear a money clue, you control the *depth of sharing* through your focus on the variables indicated on the "Measure the Depth of Sharing Chart."

Heart Level		**Head Level**
Personal	←→	**Non-Personal**
Specific	←→	**General**

Measure the Depth of Sharing Chart

If you respond to the heart-level column on this chart in a warm, personal way and specifically address what is communicated, the customer will tend to talk on a deeper level and give you more useful information. If you respond to the head level column in a non-personal, standoffish way with general comments, interaction will probably remain at a surface level.

Closely observe how the person opens up or closes down the line of communication. If the person shuts down because you have gone too deep too quickly, shift the conversation to non-personal, general talk for a few minutes.

You decide where to focus, depending on how deep you want to go. Obviously, if you focus on the heart level the person will tend to go deeper. Where you focus depends on your objective at that moment.

You don't always have to respond to clues. There are times when you can't effectively respond on a heart level.

> ## Where you focus depends on your objective at that moment in your life.

You may want to respond on the head level of the "Measure the Depth of Sharing Chart" with general head-level comments if:

- Your time is extremely limited.

- You do not have the emotional energy to listen well at that moment. There are times when you are on emotional overload due to stress.

- The situation is not conducive to talk right then, such as you are in a meeting.

In those instances, especially if it is a relationship you want to cultivate, you may want to say, "I can see that you need to talk. I want to listen. However, I don't have the time or energy to listen well right now. Can we set up another time to talk, when I can listen more fully to you?" Then set up a specific time to talk.

Respond to Money Clues to Increase Profit$

Exceptional customer service depends in part on how you respond to clues to understand the customer's point of view. It's not enough to service customers; you have to care about them. When you respond appropriately, you help the customer feel comfortable to communicate. Here are four key ways to respond to clues, that we will look at in detail:

1. Silence

2. Questions

3. Self-Disclosure

4. Observations

Silence Reveals Clues

Silence

Silence is often a powerful way to draw a person out. If someone is talkative and needs no encouragement to converse:

- Keep quiet.

- Don't interrupt.

- Focus your attention on what he communicates.

- Use positive nonverbal signals to show the person you are listening and engaged with what he is saying. Review the "How to Listen Checklist" on page 72.

Silence must be *engaged* silence with nonverbal signs that you are listening.

Silence is like a vacuum—it tends to pull things out of the heart. But it can also cause discomfort for both of you if not used wisely. Think about this question, "How comfortable are you with silence?"

Silence is more important when others share a problem than when they share a positive experience.

> ## Using silence appropriately can be a powerful way to draw out a person.

Silence can work to your advantage or disadvantage.

Silence—The Disadvantages

- Causes the person to feel awkward if he is uncomfortable with silence

- Communicates lack of interest if your body language shouts, "I am not interested!" Look at the "Relationship Saboteurs Checklist" on page 38.

Silence—The Advantages

- Provides an opportunity for the customer to process what he thinks or feels—especially if he has a complaint.

- Demonstrates you are not in a hurry and want to help the customer.

- Shows you are relaxed and interested in the customer's real or imagined concerns.

Questions Hide or Uncover Clues

Questions

The acid test of exceptional customer service is how to uncover the customer's underlying concerns or problems. When you perceive a clue, ask a question to decide how to respond to provide customer satisfaction. However, questions can be one of the most difficult things to do *well.* Questions have the potential to:

- Open the customer up to you so you can help

- Release the person to share what he wants

- Squash the opportunity for the person to open up to you

Four Basic Types of Questions

Asking questions is a customer-service skill, just like knowing the importance of detecting nonverbal clues and listening effectively. Questions gather information so you can understand and meet the customer's needs, especially when they have not clearly communicated their concerns or desires.

Questions can be an effective communication tool. Asking questions—

- Demonstrates you are listening

- Suspends judgment or assumptions

- Reduces and clarifies misunderstandings

- Helps you learn what the customer thinks or perceives

- Demonstrates your respect for the other person

- Provides opportunities to share how your product or service will meet the customer's needs

Ask questions that relate to the customer's needs (and possibly fears) to diffuse frustration and to re-engage the customer's ability to think critically.

Closed Questions: A closed question implies there is only one right answer. If you want a person to feel safe to talk about what bothers him, avoid closed questions, which:

- Provide only one answer, such as yes or no

- Steer the conversation toward your agenda

- Pressure the person for an answer, so he complies, whether he wants to or not

- Divert the attention of the conversation away from the person's needs or complaints

- Intrude upon the person's feelings

- Close down the customer's ability to feel safe with you

> ## If you want a person to feel safe to talk about what is below the surface, avoid closed questions.

Closed questions can be very effective when you want to guide or control the conversation. However, they are not effective for getting the customer to share his inner thoughts and desires.

Some examples of closed questions include:

- Where did you see our ad?

- How much do you want to spend?

- Are you ready to purchase our product or service?

- Have you ever used our product or service?

- How soon do you need this?

Open Questions. Open questions allow the person to provide more than one possible answer. Depending upon the comfort level of the person, he may communicate the answer or opinion he really holds. Open questions:

- Demand a reply, although much less so than a closed question

- Allow the customer to answer without feeling pressured

- Open the door to freedom of expression

- Direct a person's thoughts and words

Some examples of open questions include:

- What is it about our product or services that concerns you?

- How will you use the product or service? (This could be a closed question if they only have one specific answer.)

- How can I help you?

- What do you need resolve this?

**While customers describe their frustrations or concerns, don't ask unrelated questions.
Be quiet and listen. Why?
They will give you important information.
Don't break their flow by interrupting them.**

Look at this list of questions. Which are open and which are closed? See Appendix C: Answer Key for correct answers.

☐ Open ☐ Closed How much do you want to spend?

☐ Open ☐ Closed What else would you like to tell me?

☐ Open ☐ Closed How many years have you used our product?

☐ Open ☐ Closed What happened when you said that?

☐ Open ☐ Closed How can I help?

☐ Open ☐ Closed What monthly payment can you afford?

☐ Open ☐ Closed What can we do to make this right for you?

☐ Open ☐ Closed Why did you do that?

☐ Open ☐ Closed Where do you store our product?

☐ Open ☐ Closed Did you try what we suggested?

☐ Open ☐ Closed I'm interested in your feedback. Can you tell me why you believe that?

Invitation Questions. Invitation questions invite a person to talk freely. Note, that they are a type of open questions. These questions help you get the results you want. Invitation questions effectively allow a person to communicate:

- facts

- ideas

- feelings

- opinions

- thoughts

- solutions

- anything lying beneath the surface

Invitation questions invite a person to talk freely.

Examples of invitation questions include:

- How are things going now?

- Would you like me to listen to you?

- Would you like to talk more about that?

- What has been going on since our last conversation?

- What are some of the difficulties you are facing right now with our services or products?

I Wonder Questions. "I wonder" questions gently invite the person to continue talking, but do not make the person feel pressured to reveal more than he wants. Examples include:

- I wonder what we can do to help you?

- I wonder when it will ever get resolved?

- I wonder how you ever got through that?

- I wonder what would have happened if you hadn't explained that?

Asking questions can work to your advantage or disadvantage.

Questions: The Disadvantages

These are some *possible* disadvantages. Sometimes questions can:

- Imply superiority

- Pressure a person to respond

- Inhibit personal response and openness

- Violate a person's control over self-disclosure

Questions: The Advantages

Here are some potential advantages of good questions:

- Elicit information quickly

- Provide an opportunity for a person to respond easily, because he has a specific question to answer

Sharing Clues—Self-Disclosure

Self-Disclosure

The third way to respond to clues is to say how you feel, think, and react to the clue, as well as sharing your similar experiences. Self-disclosure is a subtle but effective way to respond, especially when combined with other responses. Avoiding detachment brings you personally into the other person's experience. However, don't reroute the conversation with self-disclosure.

Be authentic. Customers will quickly tune you out if they suspect a hidden agenda.

Self-disclosure:

- Tells how the issues affect you

- Shares similar experiences

- Divulges what you know or do not know

- Communicates empathy, understanding and caring

- Finds common ground with the customer rather than focusing on differences

- Reveals how you feel, think and react to the other person

- Relates how you might react to the event described by another person

Self-disclosure can be a powerful way to draw a person out, but special care must be taken not to change the focus of the conversation to yourself. Only *briefly* talk about your experience, then bring the dialog back to your customer with a question or comment. When telling your experience, a good rule of thumb is to limit your stories to a maximum of two to three sentences.

Often it helps to follow up self-disclosure with a question or observation that relates to the self-disclosure.

> ## The third way to respond to clues is to say how you feel, think, and react to the clue, as well as sharing your own similar experiences.

There are four ways to use self-disclosure with one of the other responses in italics:

Knowledge—Discovering More. Knowledge is what you know or do not know about the person and the situation. Ways to manifest compassion and to connect with the other person include expressions such as:

- I didn't know that.

- I can't imagine what that would be like. *It had to be an incredible experience.*

- I wasn't aware of what happened to you. *Would you like to talk more about it?*

- I knew you were going through a difficult time, but I never dreamed it was that tough.

Feelings—Sensing the Heart. When you acknowledge someone's feelings, you let him know you recognize how difficult his experience has been or you share in his joy. To verbally note the person's feelings, exceptional customer service expresses kindness, affirmations and words that encourage.

- I am so sorry.

- It really hurts me to hear that.

- I'm amazed you held up under such pressure. *What helped you keep going?*

- *It is so exciting to hear what has been happening in your life.* I would love to hear more.

- It makes me sad to hear how hard this has been for you. *You have really suffered a lot this past year.*

Common Ground—Ties that Bind. Sharing a common experience validates what the other person feels or thinks. Here are some examples:

- That happened to me once.

- I remember when that happened to me. It was wonderful. *You must be thrilled.*

Other possible reactions:

- I would be angry too if I saw that happen.

- I can hardly believe all you have been through.

- That kind of thing has never happened to me. *What was it like?*

- If that happened to me, I would probably be crushed. *How are you dealing with it?*

Using Self-Disclosure can have both advantages and disadvantages.

Self-disclosure—The Disadvantages

The following are some *possible* disadvantages of self disclosure:

- Changes the focus from the other person to you

- Distracts if you go on and on telling your stories

- Inhibits further disclosure, if you show shock, anger or judging

Self-disclosure—The Advantages

Here are some possible advantages of self disclosure:

- Communicates empathy

- Encourages the other person to disclose more

- Helps the other person know you understand and are involved

- Demonstrates your honesty, openness, transparency, and vulnerability

- Builds ongoing rapport

Observations—Getting Inside the Clue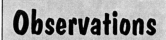

Observations are personal responses to what the person has just said. They are tentative remarks you make about what you think the customer thinks and feels. They can be communicated from a heart level, head level or a combination of both.

Self-disclosure focuses on "me and my experience." Observations focus on the other person to whom you are talking. They use "you and your experience."

The other person's responses to effective observations may:

- Make the person feel safe, not pressured

- Invite the person to talk more about what they really think or feel

Below are some effective ways to use observations. Again, you can use a question or self-disclosure to follow up.

> ## An observation can be communicated from a heart level or the head level, or a combination of both.

"It sounds like…"

- …that was a wonderful experience for you.

- …you almost didn't make it through. *What was it like for you?*

- …you are doing much more than you can handle. *You must be exhausted.*

- …your father's cancer is really difficult for you to accept. *It would be hard for me, too.*

"You must have…"

- …been really excited and thrilled. *Can you tell me more?*

- …gone through incredible stress during that time. *I wonder how you coped with it.*

> ## Observations are personal responses to what the person has just said.

"That must have…"

- …caused your entire family terrible pain. *I wonder how you survived?*

- …been one of the best experiences of your life. *I would love to hear more about it.*

"What a…"

- …great time that was for you! *Can you tell me more about it?*

- …thrill that your family is doing so well! *You must be amazed.*

"You really…"

- …have gone through so much. *I am proud of you.*

- …seem to have met the challenges of that situation.

- …seem concerned about your job right now. *How can I help you?*

Other examples:

- You have a point.

- That must be very encouraging.

- Your children must be struggling during this transition time. *What have you found helpful as you try to assist them?*

Observations can have both advantages and Disadvantages

Observations—The Disadvantages

Too many observations can:

- Make you sound like a counselor

- Inhibit the other person from resolving his problems and to come up with his solutions

Observations—The Advantages

Look at the potential advantages of appropriate observations:

- Communicate empathy

- Express understanding

- Allow the person freedom regarding what he wants to say

- Free the person to decide how deeply he wants to communicate

A True-to-Life Story: Motivate the Skeptical to Make $$$$

Bob is a salesperson for the most successful roofing company in the city. He has an appointment with Janice, who wants an estimate for a new roof.

When Bob arrives at Janice's home, he finds she is hesitant to make a decision. She tells him the names of two other companies that have already given her bids for the work. From experience, he knows his price will be the highest estimate of the three. He also senses she doesn't want to commit.

Bob asks her, "How old is your existing roof?"

"I'm not really sure. My husband always took care of those things. I think he said it needed to be replaced this year."

Bob asks, "Why isn't your husband handling this matter?"

"My husband died six months ago," she replies.

He listens attentively as she talks about her husband. Then he asks, "What has it been like for you to suddenly take on total responsibility for the upkeep of the house?"

"I feel overwhelmed trying to take care of all the household tasks my husband used to handle. I've contemplated selling the house, because of the upkeep. But I love this place too much."

Bob thoroughly understands her situation. "I lost my wife a few years ago. I remember how overwhelmed I felt trying to take care of my children's needs and work, too. It's tough managing your normal role and taking on that of your spouse, too. You've done an exceptional job—the house looks great. I'm sure you'll be able to make whatever decisions need to be made about the house."

Bob evaluates the condition of her roof and then tells her, "Your roof could be replaced. However, it's not critical to do it immediately. If you would feel more comfortable waiting a little while before you decide to replace the roof, it will be fine."

Bob leaves his proposal, not expecting to hear from Janice again. But a week later, she calls and tells him she wants his company to replace her roof—even though their costs are higher than the other companies who provided estimates. Replacing the roof on Janice's large home pays Bob a $1000 commission.

Bob used the following questions:

    a. "How old is your existing roof?"

    b. "Why isn't your husband handling this matter?"

    c. "What has it been like, suddenly taking on total responsibility for the upkeep of the house?"

Bob used the following self-disclosure:

    a. "I lost my wife a few years ago. I remember how overwhelmed I felt trying to take care of my children's needs and work, too.

    b. "I can understand how difficult it must be for you to make such a large financial decision about your home alone, when you're accustomed to having your husband make the decisions."

Bob used the following observations:

    a. "It's tough managing your normal role and taking on that of your spouse, too."

    b. "You've done an exceptional job—the house looks great."

    c. "I'm sure you'll be able to make whatever decisions need to be made about the house."

Think About It:

- Was it worth Bob's time to listen to Janice and act on his instinct that she felt indecisive?

- Was it worth taking a little extra time to build rapport rather than pressure Janice to make an extra $1000?

- If Bob hadn't known how to build rapport, he would have lost a significant amount of money for the company. Would it be worth training your employees in these skills so they make you more money?

Core Beliefs about Establishing Rapport

Your core beliefs determine how you live your life. If you didn't read the "Core Beliefs Dramatically Affect Your Profits" section on page 21, please review it now. It will help you understand this section.

Summary: A core belief is *a firmly held conviction that consistently motivates my behavior.*

Belief + Consistent Action = Core Belief

> ### Core Belief #1
> ### Responding appropriately to clues allows customers to open up and share what they really want.

Think about Core Belief #1 and answer the following questions:

1. What does this core belief mean to your bottom line?

2. How can responding to clues open lines of communication?

3. How do you normally respond to clues?

4. What could you change to provide exceptional customer service?

> ## Core Belief #2
> ## To focus on others, I need to set aside my own agenda.

Think about Core Belief #2 and answer the following questions:

1. What does this mean to you in your job, career or business?

2. How could focusing on others increase your productivity or profits?

3. Do you normally focus on others or on your agenda? Explain.

4. What could you change in relation to this core belief that will help your business?

What Would I Do to Increase My Profits?

Look at the following true-to-life stories. Then answer the questions following them.

1. Sam, a small-business owner, wants to buy equipment for his landscaping business. He comes into Sharon's business to buy five lawn tractors. Sharon has several other customers waiting for help. Sam sighs, "I wish we had a little more cash flow." Sharon tells Sam she recognizes that owning a business can be difficult financially. She listens as he tells her more about his business. Sam lets it slip that if he could afford it, he could use seven tractors instead of five. However, seven tractors are not in his budget right now.

   Sharon shows Sam corporate discounts available when customers purchase six or more pieces of equipment. With the volume discounts and low-interest financing, it will cost Sam very little more to buy seven tractors than five.

   a. If you have other customers waiting, how would you normally respond to this situation? What have you learned from this chapter that could help you respond better?

   b. What clue did Sam provide to Sharon? Review "Respond to Money Clues for Increased Profit$," starting on page 92. List six ways Sharon could respond to Sam.

   c. How can you prepare yourself to handle a situation like this?

   d. What do you think the outcome might be if Sharon responds to Sam to show that she is interested in his business? What might the outcome be if Sharon responds impatiently and fails to build rapport with Sam?

2. Jack, a car salesman, works with Katrina to replace her worn-out minivan. She makes an offhand comment about how minivans are so "Soccer Mom." They don't project the image she prefers. She longs for something more stylish, but can't afford to spend more.

Jack discovers she has three children, so she needs space. He walks her to their pre-owned SUV's and shows her a stylish two-year-old SUV. It sells for slightly more than the new "Soccer Mom" minivan. Jack asks if she likes the SUV, and how she would feel about buying a pre-owned vehicle. He says, "How you feel about what you drive is important. The SUV has low mileage and is in great condition."

a.   How would you normally respond to Katrina's "Soccer Mom" comment?

b.   What have you learned from this chapter that could help you respond better?

c.   What clue did Katrina give?

d.   Look back over "Respond to Money Clues for Increased Profit$," starting on page 92. What are six ways Jack could respond to draw her out?

e.   What might you need to do to prepare yourself to handle a situation like this?

f.   What do you think the outcome might be if Jack responds to Katrina showing that he cares about her opinion?

3. Karen is a salesperson for a large wrapping-paper company. She does phone sales with schools who sell her company's products as a fundraiser. Jackie, one school's PTA president, just received her order. More than 200 rolls of paper must be replaced, because they are badly damaged.

Since it is the last day to make quota for the month, Karen is busy. Jackie explains that the parents are anxious to get their paper. Jackie says, "I knew we should have changed vendors this year. The PTA board is going to be angry at me." Using questions, self-disclosure and observations, Karen begins to understand Jackie's frustration. She learned that Jackie's school has used their company for ten years. However, they have had trouble with their order for the last three years. The PTA board encouraged Jackie to change vendors, but she chose to remain loyal to the company.

a. How would you normally respond to this situation?

b. What have you learned from this chapter that could help you respond better?

c. What clue did Jackie give?

d. Look back over "Respond to Money Clues for Increased Profit$," starting on page 92. What are six ways you could respond to draw her out?

e. What might you need to do to prepare yourself to handle a similar situation?

f. What do you think the outcome might be if Karen responds to Jackie to show she cares about Jackie's problem and appreciates that she remained loyal to the company?

How Am I at Establishing
Two-Way Communication?

Consider how effectively you build rapport with customers and
coworkers when they send up meaningful clues.
Use this scale to indicate your responses.
You may use a separate sheet to write your answers.

1 = Hardly ever
2 = Occasionally
3 = Sometimes
4 = Often
5 = Nearly always

Clients   Coworkers

_____   _____   1. When a person sends up *nonverbal* clues, I recognize and
respond to them.

_____   _____   2. I readily recognize and respond to the *verbal* clues others send
up.

_____   _____   3. I resist turning the subject to my interests, and try to focus on
the other person's pursuits.

_____   _____   4. When trying to draw someone out, I ask open questions rather
than closed questions.

_____   _____   5. When others speak from the heart, I allow them to talk about
whatever they want.

_____ _____ 6. I avoid asking questions just to satisfy my curiosity.

_____ _____ 7. I offer observations not only about facts, but also about the person's responses and possible emotional reactions to the facts.

_____ _____ 8. I consciously choose to respond on a personal level when I sense a person wants to go deeper.

_____ _____ 9. When people talk with me from the heart, I interact   with them and gently try to draw them out further.

_____ _____ 10. I express my thoughts and feelings about what a person says to encourage him to talk more.

_____ _____ 11. I am sensitive to how deep a person is going and how quickly, and try to adjust my responses to keep him from plunging too deeply to quickly.

_____ _____ 12. I avoid trying to pressure or manipulate others to talk more deeply than they are ready to go.

_____ _____ 13. My responses are balanced, with an appropriate mixture of silence, questions, self-disclosure, and   observations.

_____ _____ 14. I am sensitive to when the person needs silence, and comfortably wait for him to continue.

_____ _____ 15. When someone freely shares from the heart, I listen attentively without interrupting.

Look over your responses to *How Am I at Establishing Two-Way Communication?*

1. **Congratulate yourself!** Did you score a 1 or a 2 in any of the situations? You are doing great!

2. **Needs Improvement.** Did you score a 3? Once you have improved the 4's and 5's, work on the 3's. If you scored a 4 or 5—

    a. Come up with an action plan to improve each area of concern.

    b. Choose one or two to begin working on right now. Which one will you start with?

3. **Talk with someone who will hold you accountable.**

    a. Who will you talk to?

    b. When will you call?

Opportunities for Growth

Note: Choose the opportunities below that you believe will be most profitable for your job, career or productivity. Choose one or two areas to start on, because trying to change in too many areas at one time can be overwhelming.

1. Over the next two weeks, when someone begins to talk with you:

   a. Ask yourself, "What level is this person on?"

   b. Consciously try to respond on the same level.

   c. Keep a list of what you did and how it affected the person talking to you.

2. Review this chapter a few times to remind yourself how to build rapport quickly.

   a. What stands out to you as you read this chapter again?

   b. What areas do you need to improve?

3. When someone shares with you on a heart level:

   a. Seek to deliberately draw him out.

   b. Consciously watch for verbal and nonverbal "clues."

   c. Ask only a few broad questions.

   d. Offer appropriate self-disclosure.

   e. Make observations.

f.   Take a few minutes afterwards to review how well you did. Evaluate what you would like to do differently the next time.

4. Go over your results again on "How Am I at Establishing Two-Way Communication?" Begin working on one or two areas where you see a need for growth. You may want to discuss these with a close friend or coworker.

5. Ask a coworker or a close friend how he would like you to respond differently when he wants to be drawn out or when there is a heart-level issue that needs to be discussed. You may want to talk specifically about how well you are doing with silence, questions, self-disclosure, and observations.

6. What are a few phrases from self-disclosure and observations that you can begin to use immediately with customers and coworkers? Memorize them so you'll be ready to use them to draw out your next customer.

    a. Self-Disclosure

    b. Observations

7. Practice Makes Profit$: The skills in this chapter do not come naturally for most people. To use them skillfully they need practice. The training DVD that goes with this chapter has a demonstration, *How to Establish Two-Way Communication*. It comes with a packet of information to help you get the most from watching it. It shows you how to practice the skills you learned in this chapter. Practice of the skills is imperative for your success in your job or business. You can obtain the DVD at www.SuccessBooks.info.Find a friend, coworker or family member to practice with regularly.

    a. Take turns giving verbal and nonverbal clues and responding to them.

    b. After practicing, give each other feedback on what worked and what could be improved.

   c. Who will you invite to practice this skill with you? When will you invite him?

8. Recognizing and responding to clues has an incredible potential to increase your effectiveness and productivity. How can you use this skill to maximize your exceptional customer service with each of the following groups of people?
   a. Potential Customers

   a. Repeat customers or customers who have a problem

   b. Coworkers or others you work with in business

   c. Business partners (including potential partners)

9. Turn to "Snapshots" at the end of this manual. Write down on that page, or in a journal, one or two things you want to work on from this chapter.

4

How to Empower People to Solve Their Problems

Effective problem solving comes before a decision to buy.

Many business owners spend much of their time solving problems for their employees and customers. When you train your employees to help each other and their customers solve problems, you work load will decrease and your profits will increase. Because customer-service representatives constantly interact with the public, problem-solving skills are crucial to provide exceptional customer service.

"Today's businesses must be prepared to solve their customers' important problems. People able to solve customer problems on a continuing basis become trusted advisers," says Garry Duncan, principal of Denver-based Leadership Connections, a sales-training company. Customers want to work with businesses that consistently provide unique solutions to their problems, and help them to solve their issues.

When an employee, coworker, customer, family member, or friend asks, "What do you think I should do about...?" then goes on to describe his struggle—what is your first reaction? You believe you can relate to the situation, because you experienced something similar. Or do you give pat answers to his problem because of training you've received at work.

> **Customers want to work with businesses that consistently provide unique solutions to their problems, and help them to solve their issues.**

You may want to offer advice on how to fix the situation. After all, you experienced it, too. If the dilemma is only a "head-level" issue, your advice may be helpful.

However, if your customer's problem is a deeper, "heart-level" issue, what he revealed to you is probably only the tip of the iceberg. To dig below the surface to undercover the core problem requires your best listening and rapport-building skills to ensure a positive outcome for the customer and for you.

Although listening is the foundation of effective customer service, listening alone may not be enough. People often want and need *practical solutions* to their problems.

When a customer or coworker is ready to explore solutions, ask yourself these questions:

- Is my advice what he *really* needs?

- Will my recommendations empower him to mature?

- Will my management of his problem lead to the best solution for him?

- Would I be most effective by helping him look into his options?

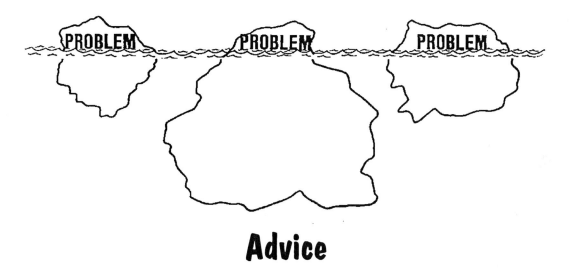

Advice

When someone comes to you with problems, are you tempted to give answers based on what the person tells you? Telling someone how to act, think or feel can be helpful. But it can also backfire. Often a person shares a surface problem—not the core issue.

When someone asks for advice, watch and listen for money clues—verbal and nonverbal signs—that the person has a deeper issue he needs to resolve.

When the person talks from a heart level, advice should be the last resort! No matter how much we listen, we will never know more than the tip of the iceberg. The person with the problem will always know more than we do.

This chapter gives a powerful skill to use with "inside" and "outside" customers. We can have a powerful effect on the "bottom line" if we create an atmosphere within our organizations, where people help each other solve their problems, rather than just giving advice. Employees will feel you care for them and they are more likely to implement changes if they have come up with the solutions themselves, rather than being told exactly what they must do.

Advice Can Be a Robber

If advice is a substitute for listening, advice robs the other person of:

> **Advice is:**
> **Telling another person**
> - **What to do**
> - **How to think**
> - **What to feel**

- caring

- true understanding

- the ability to grow in the skills to work through problems

- a safe, creative atmosphere where he can explore his options

Authentic caring respects another person's freedom to make decisions that have the potential to produce success *or* failure. When you respond by telling him what you think he should do, it is your solution, not his. He is robbed of the opportunity to find creative answers.

The ability to explore options with others is a vital customer-service skill. It enables you to stimulate creative thinking in your customer or coworker to discover a solution to his problems. The goal is to encourage him to apply one or more possibilities to achieve an adequate resolution.

> **Authentic caring respects another person's freedom to make decisions that have the potential to produce success or failure.**

What are the results for your business if you use this interactive process?

- Even if your customer's immediate solution does not involve you, he will come back to you when he needs to make a purchase, because you have gained his trust.

- He will tell others about you. I've received many quality referrals from individuals who I helped find their solutions and I didn't get paid one penny from them. Yet they sent friends to me who have spent a lot of money. I've proven to them that I have their best interests at heart—it's not just about making money.

- You will make more profits for your business because customers and coworkers know you are trustworthy and are not just out to make money.

Exploring options takes longer than giving or receiving advice, but the results are far more effective. When you help someone explore his options, he benefits by:

- Discovering answers to his problems

- Providing the opportunity for him to carefully consider all of his options

- Pursuing the solutions he discovers

- Learning how to creatively resolve future problematic situations

> ## The ability to explore options with others is a vital customer-service skill.

Supporting a person to find answers for himself does the following:

- Builds his confidence

- Promotes his mature problem-solving skills

- Encourages you to work with him toward a more rewarding outcome

- Equips the person with better skills for problem solving

Often people need *more* than just a solution to one problem. They need better skills in problem solving.

Solving Your Problems

If you struggle with a situation or problem, follow the steps lined out in this chapter to explore your options to discover solutions to your own problems. It is a productive way to examine, brainstorm, and resolve your difficulties.

You can either—

- Ask someone you trust to work through the steps in this chapter with you

- Work through the steps on your own

Timing—The Key to Exploring Options

Timing in exploring options is crucial. It is important to make sure an individual is ready to explore his options to resolve a dilemma. If he has not adequately processed through his situation, he needs the opportunity to:

- Talk about his problems and be heard on a heart level

- Receive understanding, acceptance and encouragement

- Sort any cloudy thinking

- Perceive his situation clearly after talking freely in an accepting, respectful and understanding relationship

- Catch sight of viable solutions

> **Develop your sensory. This is the skill of fine-tuning your senses, so you can observe and hear what is going on in the quality of your communication. This requires some effort.**
> Bill Twyford, *Shut Up! And Stick to the Script*

The individual may not even know the real problem. Therefore, it is important to encourage him to verbally process what he thinks and feels, before initiating the exploration of solutions.

How do you assist a person to be ready to effectively solve his own problems? As an outsider, you can't understand the total situation. If the person asks for solutions before adequately discussing it, your advice may be of little value or even harmful. To help the individual and yourself gain a more realistic grasp of the total picture, encourage him to talk out the situation in detail:

- Say, "Tell me more about the situation."

- Listen quietly as the person details the problem, so you can understand the whole situation.

- Ask relevant questions to get him to talk about his thoughts, feelings, attitudes, and wants. Review "Four Basic Types of Questions" starting on page 94. Then listen to how he answers.

- Use self-disclosure and observations to help him tell you what he really wants and desires. Review the sections on self-disclosure and observations in chapter three of this book. Then keep quiet so he can talk.

> ## If you give advice before a person adequately talks out the issue, your advice may be of little value or even harmful.

As he talks from the heart, he will begin to quietly transition towards the need to find solutions. Throughout this process, remain empathetic.

In many businesses, we can show exceptional customer service by walking our customers through the steps of this skill when they have a problem. This shows we care about them and don't want to just give them quick advice.

There are times when advice is the best solution: for example, if the customer's problem has a specific solution and your company offers a solution to that problem.

Outstanding customer service involves going the extra mile—listening, empathizing, reassuring, and guiding the customer to find a solution. A lost or dissatisfied customer is a profit gain for your competitor. If you can't help a customer resolve his problem and do business with you, he will turn to your competition. Avoid delivering your customer to the competition through poor communication. Keep your career and business strong through extraordinary customer service.

Seven Steps to Open the Door to Solutions

When you sense the timing is right for your customer or coworker to explore his alternatives, walk through the process below with him. Not every step is required for every situation, especially number four.

These steps take time, but will help you excel in your internal and external customer service. Often customers need more than just a product or service. If you listen and help them solve problems, you will have customers committed for life.

> **Often customers need more than just a product or service.**
> **If you listen and help them solve problems, you will have customers committed for life.**

The following steps are effective when your customer or coworker—

- Has a problem with your products or services

- Has a problem that your product or service can help

- Has an unrelated problem. You can build trust and develop a committed customer just by helping him work through his problem

Walk your customer through these steps to identify solutions to the problem:

Step 1   *Explore the options he has already tried.* Ask:

- What options have you already tried?

- What happened when you tried that?

- What problems did you experience?

- What were the positive outcomes?

- How do you feel about that experience?

- How does the outcome affect your willingness to try that again?

When you sense the timing is right and the individual is ready to explore his alternatives, walk through this process with the person.

Step 2   *What options have you thought about but not tried?* Try to understand the total range of options he has considered and also why he has not tried them. It is important to recognize:

- how trapped he may feel

- what alternative solutions he has or has not considered

- what fears he may have to move ahead with a solution

Step 3 *What are some new options that can be considered?* Guide him to think about other possible solutions:

- Do not dismiss any ideas.

- Brainstorm creative solutions.

- Encourage him to think "outside the box."

- Suggest specific areas of the problem to attack.

- Think of new ways to think about the situation, problem or solution.

> **Companies that don't deliver exceptional customer service will be crowded out of the marketplace.**

Step 4 *What options do you have to offer?* This is your opportunity to share some new options. However, this step is often not needed. If the individual has investigated many old, untried and new options, you may not need to offer any of your solutions. But if he is stuck or his solutions are not viable, suggest ideas for his consideration.

Step 5 *What are the pros and cons of each viable option?*

- Ask him to consider the positive and negative consequences of each option he seriously considers.

- Provide feedback regarding his perception of reality.

- If the person is too optimistic or pessimistic, help him maintain balance.

Step 6   ***What are the best options to put into action?*** Avoid pressuring him to make an immediate choice, unless it is absolutely necessary.

- If he is unwilling to take action, help him talk through any feelings of reluctance or fear.

- Assist him to outline a step-by-step process to clarify where to begin and how to follow through.

- The solutions the individual selects must be his choice, not yours.

- Try to come to a clear understanding of when and how he will put the options into practice.

Step 7   *Follow up.*

- Invite the person to be accountable to you.

- Obtain a commitment for the option he will employ and when.

- Ask him to let you know when he has applied the option and what happens as a result.

- Or, set a specific date to get back with him.

What Happens If...

- *An option didn't work?* Find out what the individual did. Uncover the reasons why it didn't work.

- *A viable option wasn't tried?* What are the reasons the individual didn't work on it? If excuses are offered, gently find out if he really wants a solution. Perhaps the individual receives something from the problem. The "pay-off" may be that the individual enjoys self-pity more than freedom from the problem.

- *Fears and other blocks prevent him from applying the options?* Help him look at what hinders him from taking action. Is his fear of confronting a person more powerful than resolving the problem? Talk through possible ways to overcome fear. If he continues to procrastinate or fails to follow through, then readdress his fears. Brainstorm ways to overcome putting off taking action in the future.

- *The options worked?* Review with him what he has learned to integrate the actions he initiated, so he can apply the process to resolve future difficulties. Reinforce and affirm the successful principles he employed.

> **"Once you have developed your sensory—
> your awareness to notice even the smallest changes
> in the people with whom you are dealing—
> the more you will be able to realize when their state
> of mind changes."**
> **—Bill Twyford,** *Shut Up! And Stick to the Script*

Other Issues that May Cloud the Picture

Is confrontation needed? It may become evident that the person's problem involves other issues. Before a resolution is explored, confrontation may be necessary. Address inappropriate attitudes or behaviors, so the issue can be resolved. Stay positive. Avoid negative words like—

- can't

- won't

- not

- shouldn't

- don't

Are your issues part of the solution or part of the problem? It is important to recognize when your personal issues influence an encounter with another person. It's important to identify emotional responses that interfere with exceptional customer service. To effectively help others explore options, answer these questions honestly:

Yes No: Does the problem feel "too close?"

Yes No: Am I doing this so I can feel needed?

Yes No: Am I helping this person so I will feel important?

Yes No: Do I lose objectivity when listening to the other person's problem?

If you answered "yes" to any of these questions, explore ways to resolve your issues, for your emotional health and for the benefit of others.

Steer Clear of These Common Pitfalls

Before you participate in the process to help your customers or coworkers solve their problems, evaluate common ways you might be tempted to respond. Your responses and evaluations are critical to success in this process. Review and avoid these common pitfalls:

Pitfall #1:   **You assume the first problem is the real problem.**

Sometimes a person will bring up a less threatening issue to see how you react. If the person feels safe, he will proceed to communicate more deeply.

Pitfall #2:   **You confuse the symptoms with the root problem.**

What the individual believes to be the root problem may only be a symptom. Often pain itself is seen as the problem. However, pain can be the symptom of unresolved grief, anger or self-hate. The symptom may be remotely related or totally unrelated.

Pitfall #3:   **You make firmly-held assumptions too quickly.**

It is normal to make assumptions right away. However, forming an opinion too quickly can hinder the process. Be aware of your first impressions. Hold them loosely. Explore your perceptions for accuracy. Be careful not to verbalize your thoughts too quickly. They can lead the discussion astray.

Pitfall #4:   **You oversimplify the cause or the solution to the problem.**

Avoid oversimplifying the problem's cause. The source of the problem may not be obvious. Often, there are multiple causes. You may think the solution is obvious. However, what worked for you may not work for him. *Remember: the goal is to assist the other person to find the right solution for him.*

Pitfall #5: You judge or condemn.

Condemnation and judgmental evaluations ring a death knell to help the person arrive at solutions. Critical judgment severely hinders your perception, closing the door to discover the root problem. Feeling condemned, the other person also slams shut the door to sharing freely.

Pitfall #6: You assume that what you hear is reality.

Look at the illustration below. A person tells you what he believes to be reality. However, his perception colors what he has just told you. As he further describes the event, you read between the lines and deduce what you believe to be reality. In actually, you are three times removed from reality!

Reality ➜ His Perception ➜ His Description ➜ Your Interpretation

A True-to-Life Story: The Rewards of Problem $olving

Note: Names have been changed at the request of the real estate agent.

Joni, a real estate agent, believes in providing exceptional customer service. She helps people find the best solution for their needs, even if she doesn't make money on the deal. She makes great money, because people know she cares about them and is not only interested in making money from them.

Jeremiah called Joni. He is behind on his house payments and wants her help to keep his house. She could have given him advice that he should just sell his house, so he can move on—after all, that's the only way she will make a profit. Instead Joni sets up an appointment to meet him.

First, Joni spends time to discover what Jeremiah's situation is, using the principles from chapter three. She finds:

1. He lost his job three months before.

2. His wife left him two months ago.

3. He is raising his five-year-old son on his own.

4. He really doesn't want to keep his house. He just wants to be out from under the stress that it brings.

5. He owes more on the house than it is worth.

Then Joni asks Jeremiah a series of questions, using the principles from this chapter. She asks him:

1. What he has already tried to remedy his house situation. She discovers all the

things he has tried, and what the results are, including:

- Looking for another job—he couldn't find one.

- Calling all the local charities to get financial help—no one could help him because he was too far behind on his payments.

- Asking relatives—none of them had any money to loan.

2. Next, she asks him what else he has thought about doing, but hasn't tried. He tells her two more options, but he doesn't like them:

- Give his house to his brother, who is not very responsible.

- Walk away from the house, but he doesn't want to totally destroy his credit.

Jeremiah keeps asking, "What should I do?" Joni has some ideas, but she wants to be sure he explores all of his options first.

3. Joni asks him if he can think of any new possible solutions. He has a couple of ideas:

- He has an uncle in another state who might be able to help him, but doesn't know if that is an option or not.

- Jeremiah realizes that he probably needs to sell his house. He knows he doesn't have any equity, but figures he can sell it anyway. He wonders if Joni can help him.

4. Joni offers some possible solutions:

- He can call his mortgage company to ask about a forbearance agreement. They talk about the fact that the company might be reticent to help him, since he doesn't have a job or any other source of income. However, it is an option to try.

- At this point, the only way Joni can help him is to work with his mortgage company to do a 'short sale[2]' on his house.

5. They review the pros and cons of his options, along with the possible consequences for each.

6. Jeremiah decides to try the following options, in this order.

   - Call his uncle to see if he can help him.

   - If his uncle can't help, he wants Joni to work on a short sale for him.

7. She follows up with Jeremiah the next week. His uncle can't help him, so he asks her to work the short sale. Joni does the short sale, and makes over $25,000. She gives Jeremiah $5000 even though he had no equity in his house.

The Results:

- Jeremiah comes up with the solution himself, so he wants to make sure it works.

- Joni signs a contract with him.

- He gives her all the paperwork needed to do the short sale.

- She is able to work out a short sale on the property.

- Joni makes over $25,000 when she sells the house a month later.

---

2 A short sale is negotiating with the mortgage company to take less than what is owed on the mortgage as payment in full.

- Jeremiah is extremely grateful because Joni saves his credit from foreclosure plus gives him $5,000 to move on, even though he doesn't have any equity in his house.

Think About It:

- Was it worth it for Joni to take a little extra time to listen to Jeremiah and ask him a few questions to help him solve his problem?

- Was it worth the two hours Joni spent working through the steps with Jeremiah to make an extra $25,000?

- How much time would you be willing to spend to make $25,000?

Core Beliefs About
Helping People Solve Problems

Your core beliefs determine how you live your life. If you didn't read the "Core Beliefs Dramatically Affect Your Profits" section on page 21, please review it now. It will help you understand this section.

Summary: A core belief is *a firmly held conviction that consistently motivates my behavior.*

Belief + Consistent Action = Core Belief

> ## Core Belief #1:
> ### When I help people solve their own problems,
> ### I build trust with them, so they *want* to work with me.

Think about Core Belief #1 and answer the following questions:

1. How can helping people solve their problems improve your job, career or business?

2. How do you normally react when someone comes to you with a problem?

3. How do you feel about helping people solve their problems?

4. In relation to this core belief, what can you change that will help you provide exceptional customer service?

> ## Core Belief #2
> ## I don't always have to have the answers
> ## to be effective with people!

When someone comes with a problem, most people think they must have all the answers, especially if they are customer-service representatives. It depends a lot on whether it's a head-level issue or a heart-level issue. If you're a computer expert and someone comes with a technical problem, it's usually your job to have the answer, or find out. Even then, at times it may be best to help them discover the solution themselves. But in heart issues, it's very different. People follow through with solutions they come up with themselves much more often than a solution they are told to implement.

Think about Core Belief #2 and answer the following questions:

1. What do you think about this core belief?

2. How do you relate to customers in light of this core belief?

3. Do you feel that you have to always give your customers, coworkers and employees advice?

4. How could your bottom line improve if you walk people through solving their problems, rather than just giving them advice?

What Would I Do to Help Solve Problems?

Look at the following true-to-life stories. Then answer the questions following them.

1. Bill is a financial advisor who sells mutual funds, IRAs and college funds. Betty and Jim come to him with a $75,000 inheritance check from Jim's mother's estate. The money was in his mother's 401k, so they're concerned about how to convert it without running into big tax complications.

   Bill explores their financial situation with them. While Betty and Jim realize that having an extra $75,000 is a good "problem," they are concerned about how to use the money to their best advantage. Bill encourages them to discuss all their financial goals, by working through the steps in this chapter.

   a. How would you normally respond in a similar situation?

   b. What have you learned from the "Seven Steps to Open the Door to Solutions" beginning on page 129 to help you respond better?

   c. How could you implement these key principles in this situation?

   d. What might you need to do to prepare yourself to handle a situation like this? Remember, situations like this often arise in customer-service arenas. Most of the time, it is easier to give advice than to work through these steps.

   e. How do you think going through the seven steps might help this couple?

g. What might be the result if Bill fails to build rapport and instead gives them quick advice?

2. Joe sells high-end plasma televisions. Max comes in to buy a plasma television. His wife reminds him that they can only afford $2000. However, the television Max really wants is $3000. How can Joe help Max solve this problem?

a. How would you normally respond to this situation?

b. What have you learned from this chapter that could help you respond better?

c. Look at the "Seven Steps to Open the Door to Solutions" beginning on page 129. How could you implement these principles in this situation?

d. What might you need to do to prepare yourself to handle a situation like this?

e. How do you think going through the seven steps might help your customer?

3. Micah works for a home-remodeling company. He arrives at the Millers' house to discuss their kitchen renovation, which he is to begin this week. Micah reviews the details to make sure he understands exactly what the job entails. However, the Millers seem distracted.

Mrs. Miller tells Micah their son has just been diagnosed with a serious illness. They realize it will cost them a lot of money to obtain medical care. They still want to remodel their kitchen so they can sell the house soon, but are unsure of their finances.

    a. How would you normally respond to this situation?

    b. What have you learned from this chapter that could help you respond better?

    c. Look at the "Seven Steps to Open the Door to Solutions" beginning on page 129. How could you implement these principles in this situation?

    d. Since it is easier to give advice, what might you need to do to prepare yourself to handle a situation like this?

    e. How do you think going through the seven steps might help the Millers?

How Successful Am I at Helping People Solve Problems?

Consider how you are at helping coworkers and customers solve their problems. Use this scale to indicate your responses.

1 = Hardly ever
2 = Occasionally
3 = Sometimes
4 = Often
5 = Nearly always

Clients   Coworkers

_____ _____   1.   When others talk about their problems, I don't feel like I have to give them answers for their problems.

_____ _____   2.   When a customer communicates on a heart level, I am willing to listen without trying to help him solve his problem.

_____ _____   3.   I help customers explore the pros and cons of their options.

_____ _____   4.   I avoid influencing others to feel or think the way I believe they should.

_____ _____   5.   Any need I have to "fix" other people's problems is under control.

_____ _____   6.   I try to discern whether others feel discouraged, hopeless, overconfident, or overly optimistic about finding solutions to their problems.

_____ _____ 7. When a person wants to solve his problem, I try to find out all he has tried to do, and how he feels about what he tried.

_____ _____ 8. I explore with others everything they have considered doing about the problem and what they think about each possibility.

_____ _____ 9. I try to help others break down complicated problems into its different components to encourage them to look at solutions to each component.

_____ _____ 10. I give my advice or possible solutions only after adequately exploring the "Seven Steps to Open the Door to Solutions"

_____ _____ 11. I avoid judging what people say they have done, have thought about doing, or new possibilities they are considering.

_____ _____ 12. I listen patiently when a customer tells me his problems. I don't begin trying to help him solve their problem until he clearly indicates he is ready.

_____ _____ 13. When someone decide to try one or more options, I help him be specific about what he will do, when, where, and how he will try the option(s).

_____ _____ 14. I set up a time to check up with him after he has finished trying his solution(s).

_____ _____ 15. If I believe a coworker is engaging in gossip or slander rather than wanting help to solve his problem, I confront him

Look over your responses to *How Am I at Helping People Solve Their Problems?*

1. **Congratulate yourself!** Did you score a 1 or a 2 in any of the situations? You are doing great!

2. **Needs Improvement.** Did you score a 3? Once you have improved the 4's and 5's, work on the 3's. If you scored a 4 or 5—

   a. In your journal, write out an action plan to improve each area of concern.

   b. Choose one or two issues to begin working on right now. Which one will you start with?

3. **Talk with someone who will hold you accountable.**

   a. Who will you talk to?

   b. When will you call?

Opportunities for Growth

Note: Choose the opportunities below that you believe will be most profitable for you. Choose one or two areas to start on, because trying to change in too many areas at one time can be overwhelming.

1. Consider any *personal issues* that may hinder you from being more effective to help your customers and coworkers solve their problems. Consider issues such as:

    a. A need to be needed.

    b. A core belief that giving advice is the best way to help people solve problems.

    c. An unhealthy need to "fix" people's problems.

    d. A fear of not having the answers for people.

    e. An attitude that you know more than the person who has the problem.

    f. Reflect:

        1) What one or two personal issues am I now aware of that I want to address?

        2) What will I begin to do to overcome them?

2. Work to become more aware of how and when you give advice and to whom. At the end of conversations, stop. Ask yourself if you gave advice when it would have been more helpful to explore options with the person or just listen well.

3. Review the "Seven Steps to Open the Door to Solutions." Memorize the steps so that you will be ready to use them when opportunities arise. Which steps are most difficult for you? Why?

> ## Seven Steps to Open the Door to Solutions
> 1. What they have already tried.
> 2. What they have thought of but not tried.
> 3. Invite them to think of new options.
> 4. Suggest some ideas of your own.
> 5. Explore pros and cons of viable options.
> 6. Help choose and apply options.
> 7. Follow up.

4. When people talk with you on a heart level about a problem, use it as an opportunity to explore options with them if they want to find solutions. After the conversation:

   a. Note how many of the steps you used.

   b. Did you give the person advice on what to do?

   c. What was the outcome?

   d. What could you do differently next time?

5. To become more skilled at exploring options, consider practicing with a family member or coworker. Use a real or hypothetical problem. Watch the training DVD that goes with this course. It gives a demonstration of how to apply the skill, as well as practical help in how to practice it. You can get the DVD at www.SuccessBooks.info.

6. Review the core beliefs from this chapter.

    a. Challenge yourself to understand what you actually believe in each area.

    b. Ask yourself, is this how you really want to act? If not, what do you need to change?

7. Turn to "Snapshots" at the end of this workbook. Write down, in your journal, one or two things you want to work on from this chapter.

5

Review: How to Apply Communication Skills to Provide Exceptional Customer Service

Review and personal assessment
of your growth in people skills
is essential to your success.

Y ou may be thinking, "Where do I want to go from here?" This course includes many topics and opportunities for you to become more successful in your job, career or business. You may feel overwhelmed by all the areas in which you need to work.

So that you can apply the skills more effectively, this chapter is designed to help you integrate the knowledge and alter old habits. This chapter may be the most difficult, but also the most helpful, part of your study. Use a separate sheet to thoughtfully respond to any questions you need more space.

> **This chapter is designed to help you integrate the knowledge and skills gained through your study of this workbook, so you can apply them more effectively.**

Assessing My Response to This Study

Consider the material and skills presented, and how you personally responded to them. Review this book, then answer the following questions.

1. Facts Presented

    a. Which topics provided me the most helpful information and insights?

    b. As I think back over these topics, what specific ideas or insights were new to me?

    c. The most important thing I learned from this study is:

2. Skills Gained

   a. Which skills especially stand out as being important to me personally and professionally?

   b. Of these skills, the one(s) I need most is/are:

   c. The new skill I got the best handle on through this study is:

3. Application

   a. What is one way you can apply some idea or insight from this course in your personal relationships, job, career, or business? For example, *Now that I realize listening is more important than advice, I plan to be more attentive and withhold unsolicited advice when customers face difficult issues, complain or feel frustrated.*

   b. One specific way I can apply a new skill in my relationships is to:

Examining My Personal Issues

In this section you will look at your personal issues. As you consider insights gained or reconfirmed about yourself from this study, carefully answer these questions.

1. **My Core Beliefs**

    a. Which of my core beliefs about interpersonal relationships have been strengthened through this study?

    b. Which core beliefs have been dropped or updated?

    c. What new core beliefs am I beginning to hold as a result of this study?

2. **My Needs and Fears**

    a. What are the needs and/or fears that have hindered me in my job, career or business of which I am now aware?

    b. Which ones do I believe I need to begin to confront?

3. **Application**

    a. How will I begin to work on one core belief, need or fear? Write one goal.

    b. What will I plan to do and when? For example, "I will talk about my need to _____ with my business partner or closest coworker and ask him to remind me when it hinders my relationships, and seek to overcome it."

Future Growth

Consider some specific ways in which you are committed to grow in the months ahead, based on your study of this book.

1. **Identifying and Overcoming Hindrances**

    a. Two or three internal factors (weaknesses or other characteristics) which hinder my ability to improve my business relationships or provide exceptional customer service are.... (For example, "difficulty concentrating, tendency to be judgmental, impatience, self-centeredness rather than other-centeredness.")

    b. Two or three behavior patterns that hinder my ability to connect better with customers and other people are... (For example, a tendency to talk rather than listen, a habit of interrupting or being too quick to give advice.)

    c. What one internal factor or behavior pattern can I overcome? What will I do and when?

2. **Commitment to Grow in Knowledge and/or Skills**

    a. What goal will I work on to continue to grow in my knowledge and/or skills to help others. For example: "Set aside two hours a week to study through this course with my spouse or coworker," or "Consciously apply listening skills with my partner for a month."

    b. Two people with whom I have a close relationship at present are:

    Person #1:

Person #2:

    c. A specific skill I will begin applying in my relationship with each of these two people is:

3. You may want to get together with a friend or coworker who has studied this book to discuss issues and practice skills.

    a.   Who will you approach for this purpose?

    b.   When will you do it?

My hope is that you will continue to grow in these skills and seek to apply what you learned through this study so all your relationships will improve—personal and professional—and your profits will multiply.

Appendices

Appendix A: Small Groups

Are you are a manager or business owner and you want your company to provide exceptional customer service so you stand above all your competition? If so, study this course with all your employees. When you do, you will notice a dramatic increase in your profits.

Read what one business owner wrote about using this book with his employees:
"Just wanted to let you know my office staff and I went through relationship killers yesterday. "Ouch!" We were surprised by the things we do without realizing it, Now that our team is aware of our "habits", we can support each other to grow beyond them. The material you provided in this course is excellent. It is a must read for anyone that deals with other people. *I highly recommend that anyone overseeing a team go through this manual together*"

The purpose of doing this study as a team is to:

1. Develop and practice communication and conflict management skills

2. Talk to others about issues of growth

3. Learn from each other

4. Develop a stronger team so you work together better and therefore increase your profits.

Each person in a group must make a commitment to keep confidential everything heard in the group. Even if you think people would not mind, do not share their stories with others, *unless they gave you* specific permission to share.

NOTE: You can receive a discount by ordering in bulk, directly from our website.

Group Discussions

Choose a leader for your group. This person can change each week, if desired.

Allow everyone to share in the group discussion, *if* they desire. Consider the following regarding personality types in groups—

- Extroverted people are naturally more talkative and eager to contribute often.
- Introverts are more reticent to share. It takes introverts longer than others to formulate their ideas.
- Silence during group discussions can be an effective way to draw out introverts.
- Extroverts feel uncomfortable during silence and will want to fill it with talk.

Individuals who find it easy to speak in groups should be encouraged to be aware of those who do not find it easy. If someone has already addressed the issue being discussed, allow others to share. Be slow to share until others have had ample opportunity to talk.

Note to Leaders

1. Do not ever call on anyone in the group unless you know that he or she wants to speak. Some people, especially introverts, are uncomfortable if they are called on to speak. Calling on people when they do not want to speak can destroy the safety in the group for that person and for others, who may be afraid you will also call on them.

2. Be certain you understand how to lead a group discussion. Success Builders International has a book, *Become a Dynamic Facilitator*, designed to help you successfully lead a small group.

3. Before your small group meets, thoroughly study the materials.

If you have questions about leading these materials in a small group, feel free to email us at Questions@SuccessBooks.info.

Appendix B: About Success Builders International

Success Builders International:

- Provides individual coaching for business leaders and customer-service representatives who want to quickly maximize their profits in any arena.

- Makes available quality materials to help individuals and groups grow in their interpersonal skills and to improve their relationships.

- Facilitates *Customer-service Communication Workshops* for businesses and individuals.

- Trains qualified individuals to effectively facilitate interactive *Customer-service Communication Workshops.*

- Provides *Sharpen Your Training Skills Workshops* to help both leaders learn to integrate effective adult learning principles into their training experience, so participants learn and retain more.

- Facilitates *De-Stress Your Life Workshops.*

If you want more information about Success Builders International, our products, or workshops, log on to our website at
www.SuccessBooks.info.

About Success Books Workshops

> "These workshops are a key feature of our leadership development architecture.
> The strong foundation, skill orientation, and adult learning approach are a powerful combination.
> Taken to heart, these workshops help people to grow in their personal lives as well as work together more effectively.
> We believe in these workshops.
> That's why we've trained a global network of facilitators."
> —Ben Sells, PhD, Director of International Center for Excellence in Leadership

Each relationship-changing workshop features:

- Practical teaching to apply good people skills in your job, career or business

- A course manual

- Demonstrations of each skill to help customer-service representatives and business leaders develop effective skills to face real problems

- Group interaction

- Skills practice to reinforce powerful tools

- Time for personal reflection for application and deep learning

Check our website for upcoming workshops that are open or to schedule a workshop for your group — www.SuccessBooks.info

Workshop Endorsements

"This is the only seminar/workshop I have ever come home from feeling like I could do what they taught because I had done it."
—Beverly, Texas

"A simple increase in knowledge about relationships isn't enough to change behavior. Practice is the key and practice is at the core of this workshop. This material applies to every area of my life."
—Phil, a Human Resources Director, Orlando, Florida.

"Every time I have the opportunity to study this material with you, I'm blown away. I truly come home refreshed and inspired. The material is so much more believable, because I can see how you apply it in your lives."
—Lee Ann, Texas

"I'm going to be different, not overnight but over the long haul. Here was a workshop that was not hype, emotions and fluff, but nuts and bolts, hammer and trowel—foundational stuff! It needs to be slow-drip learning for life-long change."
—John, Texas

"This was the best workshop I've ever attended. It transformed parts of my own personal life. It was extremely helpful for my work. The written material is marvelous."
—A nonprofit leader in Kenya

"I came here thinking this was going to help me on the job, but throughout the week it became more and more obvious that all of this applies to how I interact as a wife and mom! If you don't practice this at home, don't try to export it outside your home to your business! It was like attending a marriage-building seminar without my spouse!"
—Nancy, Kenya

"The unanimous expression was, 'Why haven't we been presented with this material before?'"
—Orman, Costa Rica

"There were many strained relationships and lack of trust among the staff, but as the topics were dealt with, a beautiful thing happened. People went to each other seeking to work through their differences and build relationships, not just among the staff, but also in marriages and families."
—Peter, Guam

> ## "This is the most helpful, practical, meaningful and applicable workshop I have EVER attended..."
> ### George, a leader in California

"This is the best course we have *ever* had at our university. It is a lot of fun and the students are really participating."
—A University Professor, Amman, Jordan

"The workshop surpassed all our expectations in the deep learning, vulnerability, and obvious change that took place before our very eyes on a daily basis. Participants and non-participants are talking about the visible positive results in meetings and personal interactions that they observed to be directly attributed to the workshop."
—Ed, Ecuador

"This material is the best training tool I've seen. I really believe in it."
—Duane, Thailand

"I have three things to say about your material:
    1) excellent
    2) Excellent
    3) EXCELLENT!!
It is definitely worth the price of the course!"
—Phil, Ecuador

Appendix C: Answer Key
For page 97

☐ Open   ☑ Closed How much do you want to spend?

☑ Open   ☐ Closed What else would you like to tell me?

☐ Open   ☑ Closed How many years have you used our product?

☑ Open   ☐ Closed What happened when you said that?

☑ Open   ☐ Closed How can I help?

☐ Open   ☑ Closed What monthly payment can you afford?

☑ Open   ☐ Closed What can we do to make this right for you?

☑ Open   ☐ Closed Why did you do that?

☐ Open   ☑ Closed Where do you store our product?

☐ Open   ☑ Closed Did you try what we suggested?

☑ Open   ☐ Closed I'm interested in your feedback. Can you tell me why you believe that?

Appendix D:
Personal Coaching for Dramatic Profits

Gaylyn Williams offers personal, one-on-one coaching and mentoring for a select group of students. She works with students through—

- Weekly phone calls

- Email

- Fax

She is dedicated to helping you be successful in your life and your business or career. Gaylyn will walk you through the scores of situations that you will encounter as a business owner or customer-service representative.

When a situation comes up, you can call, email or fax her with your question and she will help you deal with it in ways that will increase your profits.

Gaylyn offers mentoring and ongoing training for business leaders. She personally provides one-on-one coaching to walk you through every communication challenge you may face in your business as well as your personal life.

For more information about this coaching program and to see if you can qualify, please email Gaylyn at coaching@SuccessBooks.info.

Appendix E: Other Books by Author

Overcome Conflict for Maximum Success, 2006, Success Books

Harness the Power of Communication, 2006, Success Books

The Essential Communication Toolkit, 2003, Success Books

De-Stress Your Life, 2003, Success Books

Sharpen Your People Skills, 2002, Success Books

Sharpen Your Interpersonal Skills, co-authored with Ken L. Williams, PhD, 1998, Relationship Resources, Inc.

Christmas Activity Book, 1994, Standard Publishing; Reprinted in 2002 by *Readers Digest*

Children's books published by Thomas Nelson Publishers in 1994 and translated into numerous languages:
1. *Friends Around the World*
2. *Animals from the Bible*
3. *God's Wonderful World*
4. *Friends from the Bible*

The Door to Joy, coauthored with Ken L. Williams, PhD, Paperback (July 1993) Publisher: Broadman and Holman

The *Wycliffe International Cookbook*, Gaylyn Williams, Spiral Bound (March 1990) Publisher: Wycliffe Bible Translators (In its fifth printing.)

Other Books in the
Customer Service Communication Library

Overcome Conflict for Maximum Success: Book 2

Conflict is inevitable with business customers and business associates. Dealing with conflict is never easy. Discover how to turn conflict into a sales advantage.

1. **How to Manage Conflict Successfully:** When others overreact, does it drive you nuts? This chapter examines ground rules for effective conflict resolution along with a strategy to successfully manage conflict in your business.

2. **How to Confront Effectively Even When You Are Angry or Terrified:** Learn successful principles and specific skills to confront others. Discover how to control words and unconscious signals that trigger or reduce conflict.

3. **How to Respond to Verbal Attacks:** How do you respond to a verbal attack from your customer? Learn how reactions dramatically affect the outcome. Master the skills to diffuse an attack.

4. **How to Help Others Manage Conflicts:** When the customer and his relatives fight about the deal, do you feel like a piece of cheese between two rats? Learn practical strategies and mediation techniques to help others resolve conflict that will increase your sales.

Stress Less: Proven Techniques to Resolve Stress and Maximize Productivity: Book 3

Stress is a major issue for customer-service professionals. It affects you, your family, and your business or career. But it doesn't have to get you down. Discover how stress can work for—not against—you.

1. **Evaluate Your Stress and It's Affects.** Stress affects everyone differently. Learn how stress works. This chapter helps you identify your stressors. Unless you know what your stressors are and how they affect you, you can't begin to deal with them.

2. **Employ Effective Stress Management Techniques.** Discover specific strategies to manage your stress, using practical resources to lower your stress level and keep it manageable.

3. **Overcome Busyness for a Balanced Life and Business:** Equilibrium in life is essential, yet the business culture equates busyness with success. This chapter examines principles on how to maintain a balanced life. Build a strategy that works for you to put balance back into your life, so you can be more productive.

Successful Business Ethics: Book 4

Association with family, friends, customers, and other business colleagues directly affects your business reputation in the community. These critical topics can help you build standing among your peers and buyers.

1. **Gain Others Confidence in You:** How do others judge or perceive your business integrity? This chapter analyzes the qualities that can build or destroy your business reputation.

2. **Build Trust in a Distrustful World:** Gaining someone's trust is critical to close the sale and obtain referrals. Discover the words, actions, and attitudes that destroy or build people's trust in you.

3. **Maintain Your Good Reputation:** This chapter deals with maintaining your ethical and legal boundaries to preserve your personal and business reputation.

Successful Strategies to Assist Customers in Crisis: Book 5

Many stressed out or hurting customers and business associates are experiencing a significant hardship. Learn how to help customers through their struggles while increasing your profits.

1. **Building Relationships Through Active Listening**: This chapter equips you with listening and understanding tools to help those who are in crisis.

2. **Overcome Life's Losses**: People experiencing significant losses can be difficult to work with. Understanding grief fine-tunes your insight to more effectively communicate and help others.

3. **Lift People Up When Life Puts Them Down**: Reap large results from small investments of time and energy. Learn practical ways to encourage both customers and business associates. These simple, easy-to-implement ideas will cause your profits to explode.

Appendix F: Snapshots

At the end of each chapter, consider one or two things you want to take away. Note them in the appropriate section.

How to Avoid Sabotaging Your Profit$

Maximize Profit$:
How to Listen to Provide Exceptional Customer Service

How to Establish Rapport to Build Customer Loyalty

How to Empower People to Solve Their Problems

Printed in the United States
217147BV00003B/9/P

9 781432 711498

MEMORABLE
OLYMPIC GYMNASTICS
MOMENTS

BY ERIN NICKS

SportsZone

An Imprint of Abdo Publishing
abdobooks.com

abdobooks.com

Published by Abdo Publishing, a division of ABDO, PO Box 398166, Minneapolis, Minnesota 55439. Copyright © 2021 by Abdo Consulting Group, Inc. International copyrights reserved in all countries. No part of this book may be reproduced in any form without written permission from the publisher. SportsZone™ is a trademark and logo of Abdo Publishing.

Printed in the United States of America, North Mankato, Minnesota
042020
092020

THIS BOOK CONTAINS
RECYCLED MATERIALS

Cover Photo: AP Images
Interior Photos: Ed Lacey/Popperfoto/Getty Images, 4–5; AFP/Getty Images, 6; John Gaps/AP Images, 9, 22; AP Images, 11, 14; History and Art Collection/Alamy, 12; The Asahi Shimbun/Getty Images, 13; Suzanne Vlamis/AP Images, 17, 19; Lionel Cironneau/AP Images, 20; Susan Ragan/AP Images, 23; Amy Sancetta/AP Images, 24–25; Gregory Bull/AP Images, 26–27; Leonard Zhukovsky/Shutterstock Images, 29

Editor: Charly Haley
Series Designer: Megan Ellis

Library of Congress Control Number: 2019954384

Publisher's Cataloging-in-Publication Data

Names: Nicks, Erin, author.
Title: Memorable olympic gymnastics moments / by Erin Nicks
Description: Minneapolis, Minnesota : Abdo Publishing, 2021 | Series: Gymnastics zone | Includes online resources and index.
Identifiers: ISBN 9781532192388 (lib. bdg.) | ISBN 9781098210281 (ebook)
Subjects: LCSH: Gymnastics--Juvenile literature. | Olympic gymnastics--Juvenile literature. | Sports--History--Juvenile literature. | Gymnastics for children--Juvenile literature.
Classification: DDC 796.44--dc23

CONTENTS

CHAPTER 1

A PERFECT 10

When Nadia Comăneci dismounted from the uneven parallel bars after her routine, she thought she had done very well. Comăneci was competing at the 1976 Summer Olympics in Montreal, Canada. She was only 14 years old at the time. She wasn't prepared for what happened next, because it was one of the most remarkable moments in Olympic history.

Comăneci was already preparing for the next event. But then she heard the noise from the crowd. The young gymnast from Romania turned to see what all the fuss was about.

Nadia Comăneci performs on the uneven parallel bars at the 1976 Olympics.

Comăneci's eyes landed on the scoreboard. It read, "1.00."

It appeared to be the worst score an Olympic gymnast had ever seen. But it was not. It was the best score—a perfect 10. The scoreboard was not able to post "10.00" because it could only fit three numbers. Before the Olympics had started that year, the organizers were asked if the scoreboard would need to have room for four numbers. They said they did not think it was necessary. But on July 18, 1976, Comăneci

Comăneci, *right*, cheers on the podium after being awarded a gold medal.

proved them wrong. She had made history as the first gymnast to receive a perfect score at the Olympics.

Comăneci captured a total of seven perfect 10s during her time in Montreal. She was flawless in her four appearances on the uneven bars. Her other three perfect scores came on the balance beam. She won the gold medal in both events, as well as in the all-around competition. Her Romanian team won silver, and Comăneci also snagged a bronze medal for her floor routine. Her performance at the Olympics made Comăneci an international star. Her picture appeared on the covers of magazines around the world. Her name was added to the Guinness Book of World Records.

OTHER PERFECT 10s

While Comăneci got most of the attention, she was not the only gymnast to earn a perfect score during the 1976 Olympics. Nellie Kim, competing for the Soviet Union, landed a 10 for her performance on the vault, which featured one-and-a-half flips with a full twist.

Other women have also clinched perfection at the Olympics. American Mary Lou Retton scored a 10 on the vault and in her floor routine during the 1984 Summer Olympics in Los Angeles, California. Daniela Silivaş of Romania matched Comăneci's seven perfect 10s at the 1988 Olympics in Seoul, South Korea. In 1992 Romania's Lavinia Miloşovici and China's

THE FIRST MAN WITH A PERFECT 10

Aleksandr Dityatin of the Soviet Union became the first man to score a perfect 10 in Olympic competition. He was awarded the score after his vault in the all-around competition during the 1980 Olympic Games in Moscow, Russia.

Chinese gymnast Lu Li, *center*, who won gold for uneven bars and sliver for balance beam in 1992, was one of the last gymnasts to score a perfect 10 at the Olympics.

Lu Li scored some of the last 10s seen on the Olympics scoreboard.

After 2006 the scoring system for international gymnastics changed, and the perfect 10 was retired. But Comăneci's first perfect performance will remain one of the most memorable moments in both Olympic and gymnastics history.

CHAPTER 2

THE EARLY YEARS

Gymnastics has been an Olympic sport for more than 120 years. The first modern Olympic Games in 1896 included men's gymnastics. The youngest medalist in Olympic history came from those games in Athens, Greece. A 10-year-old Greek boy named Dimitrios Loundras participated in a team parallel bars event, and his group won bronze.

Stunning moments in Olympic gymnastics continued through the years. At the 1904

A gymnast performs a pommel horse routine at the first modern Olympics in 1896.

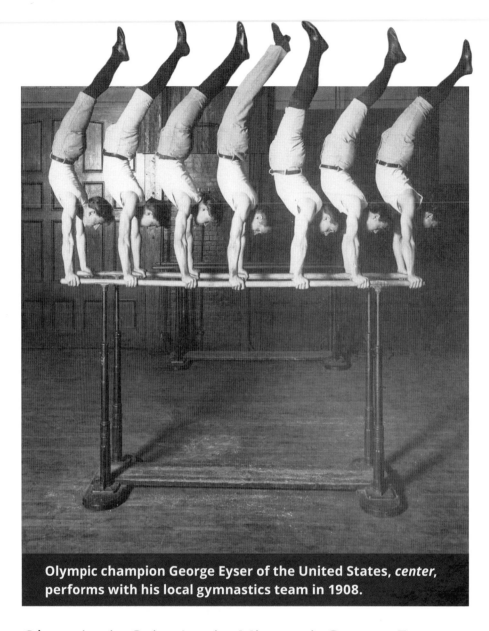

Olympic champion George Eyser of the United States, *center*, performs with his local gymnastics team in 1908.

Olympics in Saint Louis, Missouri, George Eyser of the United States won three gold medals in one day. He won these in vault, parallel bars, and rope climbing. He also won two silver medals in the combined three events and pommel horse, and he won bronze on the high bar. Part of why Eyser's wins were incredible was because he was competing on a wooden left leg. Eyser had lost his leg in a train accident.

Polina Astakhova of the Soviet Union competes on balance beam at the 1964 Olympics in Tokyo, Japan.

WOMEN ENTER THE PICTURE

Women were first allowed to compete in an all-around gymnastics event at the 1936 Olympics in Berlin, Germany. By 1952 women could also receive medals in individual events. In the 1950s, the Soviet Union became

13

Olga Korbut flips through the air.

known as the strongest country in women's gymnastics. These Soviet athletes displayed a great combination of skills. They were strong and precise. They were also graceful. These talents helped their country stay on top of the Olympic gymnastics scene from 1952 to 1992.

STELLAR SOVIET GYMNASTS

One of the Soviet Union team's amazing gymnasts was Polina Astakhova. She competed in the Olympic Games in 1956, 1960, and 1964. In that time, she won five gold, two silver, and three bronze medals, including back-to-back golds on the uneven bars.

In 1972 a Soviet gymnast named Olga Korbut gained a lot of attention for her memorable performance on the uneven bars. Korbut's historic routine included a moment where she stood on the top bar and performed a backflip. The move was so shocking that it became known as the "Korbut Flip."

NO MORE KORBUT FLIP

Korbut's famous move was eventually banned in the Olympic Code of Points rulebook because it interrupts the continuous flow required in an uneven bars routine.

CHAPTER 3

HERE COME THE AMERICANS

The world of gymnastics changed forever when Romanian coach Béla Károlyi stayed behind in the United States during an exhibition trip to New York City in 1981. Károlyi was the coach for Nadia Comăneci and the Romanian team during the 1976 Olympics. In 1982 Károlyi met Mary Lou Retton and became her coach. He also started coaching Julianne McNamara, another American gymnast. Both young women earned spots on the 1984 US Olympic team.

American Julianne McNamara performs on balance beam at the 1984 Olympics.

McNamara became the first American woman to score a perfect 10 at an Olympic gymnastics event. Her achievement came on the uneven bars. But it was Retton who became the star of the 1984 Olympics. The games were held in Los Angeles, and the American crowd went wild for the young star. Retton hit perfect scores on both the vault and the floor exercise. She was

BÉLA KÁROLYI

Béla Károlyi moved to the United States from Romania in 1981. At that time, some communist countries greatly restricted travel for their citizens. Romania was one of these. The fear was that traveling outside of communist-led countries would expose citizens to new ideas. However, some athletes and coaches were allowed to travel because communist leaders saw their talents as a way to promote their home countries. During a gymnastics tour in 1981, Károlyi took advantage of his travel abilities and defected from Romania to live in the United States.

Mary Lou Retton smiles at the end of a routine at the 1984 Olympics.

also the first American woman to win gold in the all-around event. This was even more amazing considering that Retton had undergone knee

Members of the US men's team celebrate their Olympic gold medals in 1984.

surgery six weeks before the Olympics began. Retton became an international star and an American sports hero.

US MEN'S TEAM

While Retton was the highlight of the 1984 Olympics, the US men's team also had a fantastic performance. The United States won the men's team competition for the first time in history. Gymnasts such as Peter Vidmar and Mitch Gaylord clinched several medals individually too. Vidmar won gold on the pommel horse and silver in the all-around event. Gaylord won silver on the vault. He also won bronze on the rings and parallel bars.

HIGHLIGHTS FROM BARCELONA AND ATLANTA

In 1992 Vitaly Scherbo of the Unified Team (made up of athletes from the former Soviet Union) made Olympic history in Barcelona, Spain. He won six gold medals for team competition, pommel horse, parallel bars, rings, vault, and the all-around event. He captured four gold medals in one day. Scherbo won the most medals in any event at the 1992 Olympic Games.

In 1996 the US women's team finally won gold. The Olympics took place in Atlanta, Georgia.

Vitaly Scherbo performs on the rings at the 1992 Olympics.

One of the most memorable moments involved American Kerri Strug. The 18-year-old had fallen badly after her first vault and injured her ankle The US team needed a high mark from Strug's second vault to win gold over the Russian team. Strug managed to perform a great second vault

Béla Károlyi carries an injured Kerri Strug to the podium to accept her gold medal in 1996.

and stuck the landing. She then fell to her knees in horrible pain. The Americans beat the Russians by .821 points. Károlyi carried Strug in his arms to the medal podium in front of a cheering crowd.

CHAPTER 4

BIG MOMENTS OF THE 21ST CENTURY

American gymnasts have continued to deliver memorable moments at the Olympics. At the 2004 Olympic Games in Greece, American Paul Hamm shocked the gymnastics world by beating Kim Dae-Eun of South Korea for the all-around men's title. He was the first man from the United States to win gold in that event. In his last event on the high bar, Hamm scored a 9.837, edging Kim for the

American Paul Hamm performs on the rings in 2004.

gold in the all-around event by .012 points. At the 2008 Olympics in Beijing, China, a new US men's team surprised many when it won bronze. No one on the team had ever even been in the Olympics before.

On the women's side, China grabbed its first gold medal in the team competition in 2008. Winning the title in front of its home crowd was a huge moment for the Chinese team, which beat an American squad that had been dominating the individual events. Shawn Johnson and Anastasia Liukin, both of the United States, battled against each other on beam, floor exercise, and the all-around. Liukin took the gold in the all-around, silvers on balance beam and the uneven bars, and bronze on the floor exercise. Johnson won gold on beam and silvers on the floor and in the all-round.

RAISMAN'S STUNNING LOSS

At the 2012 Olympic Games in London, England, fans were shocked when a tiebreaker kept American Aly Raisman from winning a bronze medal in the all-around event. Raisman and Aliya Mustafina of Russia were tied at 59.566 after finishing all of their events. The tiebreaker involved dropping the lowest scores and adding up the rest for

Despite losing the all-around bronze medal in a tiebreaker, Aly Raisman still took home two gold medals and one bronze from the 2012 Olympics.

each gymnast. Raisman had a score of 14.200 on the balance beam dropped. Mustafina's lowest score was 13.633, also on balance beam. The final scores left Raisman with 45.366 and Mustafina had 45.933, giving Mustafina the bronze medal.

SIMONE BILES

In 2016, Simone Biles of the United States won five medals at the Olympics in Rio de Janeiro, Brazil. She won gold in the all-around event, floor exercise, and vault, as well as a team gold medal. She also won bronze on the balance beam. Biles tied American swimmer Katie Ledecky as the most decorated female athlete at that Olympics.

MORE MEMORABLE MOMENTS

Today it is easy for gymnastics fans to relive some of the sport's most memorable moments. In the past, fans might have only caught glimpses of gymnastics events on television. Now people can watch online videos of exciting routines whenever they want. This has helped gymnastics

Simone Biles competes on balance beam in 2016, the year that she won five medals.

become more popular around the world. As the sport continues to grow, there will be many more memorable gymnastics moments at Olympic Games in the future.

GLOSSARY

ALL-AROUND

When gymnasts compete in all of the events as an individual. The all-around champion earns the most points from all the events combined.

CLINCHED

Confirmed or finalized, such as one's finish in a competition.

DISMOUNT

To land after performing on the vault, pommel horse, balance beam, high bar, uneven bars, rings, or parallel bars.

EXHIBITION

A noncompetitive event.

PODIUM

An elevated stage where athletes are awarded their medals.

POMMEL HORSE

An event in which male gymnasts balance and perform tricks on their hands on a bench covered with foam, rubber, and leather that has two plastic handles on the top (the pommels).

PRECISE

Exactly right.

TIEBREAKER

A rule put in place to decide a winner when two competitors have the same score.

MORE INFORMATION

BOOKS

Lawrence, Blythe. *Best Male Gymnasts of All Time*. Minneapolis, MN: Abdo Publishing, 2020.

Mattern, Joanne. *Simone Biles: America's Greatest Gymnast*. New York: Scholastic, Inc., 2018.

Moore, Kaitlin. *Kerri Strug and the Magnificent Seven*. New York: Random House Children Books, 2016.

ONLINE RESOURCES

Booklinks
NONFICTION NETWORK
FREE! ONLINE NONFICTION RESOURCES

To learn more about memorable Olympic gymnastics moments, please visit abdobooklinks.com or scan this QR code. These links are routinely monitored and updated to provide the most current information available.

INDEX

ABOUT THE AUTHOR

Erin Nicks is from Thunder Bay, Ontario, Canada. She has worked as a writer, newspaper columnist, and reporter for 20 years. She currently resides in Ottawa, Ontario.